Live

Your

Purpose

**A step by step guide on
how to live your best life**

Rick Heyland

ISBN-13: 978-1-7358955-1-2

Cover Design: Carolyn Sheltraw

Graphic Design: Leila Hofmeister

Text Design: Marianne Thompson

Recommendations and Insights
About Live Your Purpose

"As Rick Heyland reminds us, 'Purpose is the reason you were created; it is your ultimate why.' This terrific book not only addresses the need to develop focused purpose statements, but takes us on a practical journey to live our best lives. Full of real-world takeaways and wisdom from a highly rated management consultant and senior business leader, this gem of a book will quickly become the go-to standard for anyone looking to live a more purposeful life."

~Adrian Gostick, New York Times bestselling author, "Leading with Gratitude"

"The experience of going through Live Your Purpose was like discovering my car had four-wheel drive for the first time. Rick has distilled the wisdom of living your life with purpose into an incredibly practical and insightful book that takes you on a journey. It will leave you both challenged and inspired. Live Your Purpose is a gift from a man with a lifetime of unleashing the potential in others. Thank you, Rick."

~Jerry Weisenfelder, COO, RLG International

"The impact of Rick's message is powerful because he shares his own raw feelings, emotions, and experiences that drove him to establish his purpose at a young age. Rick delivers his first-hand personal practice and success of developing a process for continuous improvement and purpose through his fact-based, practical methods. The proof of Rick's compelling message is found in the successful outcome of his life and efforts over decades of refinement. His authentic approach is very relatable and super effective. CI4Life!"

~Bryan Schramm, COO & Co-founder, Liqid

"Excellent read! After working with Rick for over 16 years, he has always had the talent for transforming challenges into simple and inspiring solutions. This book is a perfect example! I've had the pleasure of Rick's coaching. He has helped me many times during my professional career in expanding my sense of purpose and leveraging my strengths to deliver systematic and sustainable improvements."

~Susan Sharp, Energy Executive

"Rick's distilled 31 years of living a purpose-filled life into a powerful must read. It's literally all the things I wish I knew starting my career, my family and my purpose-filled journey, all rolled into one."

~Robert Mason, Global Business Development Director, RLG International

"Writing a book is an important way for entrepreneurs to get their ideas out in the world. I read roughly 24 books a quarter and out of all the books I have read recently, yours was one of my favorites! It might actually be in my top 10 picks. The genius of your book isn't that it helps your reader figure out their purpose - it's that you provide practical ways in which a person can live their purpose to their fullest in the various facets of their life. For example, at work, with their family, etc. You also provide invaluable exercises and questions to help your reader create and focus on their purpose. Love the opportunity after each chapter to do just this. You did a great job at giving recognition to the various people that influenced your process. Not many people do that these days."

~Serafina Pupillo, Director of Legal Services, The Strategic Coach Inc.

"In Live Your Purpose, Rick shares a step-by-step success formula refined over years of continuous improvement. For years, I have enjoyed Rick's approachable style and admired his productivity and results, and with this book, I now see the pieces which together make up a powerful solution. I enjoyed the readability and organization in the book and wholeheartedly recommend it to those just starting to seek a purpose, and to those, like me, who needed a timely reminder of what matters."

~John Shewfelt, Vice President, Capability and Development, RLG International

"The book is inspirational and practical. I got motivated just by reading the first four chapters to review my life purpose.

Thank you for helping humanity and being vulnerable by sharing your purpose and this journey - which is the greatest gift you give us."

~Carina Lovato Gillenwater, Vice-President, Human Resources, Southwestern Energy

"Live Your Purpose is a gift to yourself and all whose lives you touch. Rick Heyland provides a road map to a rich and fuller life, a path to bringing joy and passion to your daily life. You will find elegant strategies for achieving your goals and turning stumbling blocks into steppingstones."

~Dr. Robert Maurer, author of "Small Steps That Can Change Your Life - The Kaizen Way"

Table of Contents

Introduction

Research shows that when people are on their deathbed, the number one regret is that they did not live their best life!

Bronnie Ware is a palliative nurse who recorded her insights on death in her book, *The Top Five Regrets of the Dying*.

Here are the top five regrets as witnessed by Ware:

1. I wish I had the courage to live a life true to myself, not the life others expected of me.

2. I wish I had not worked so hard.

3. I wish I had had the courage to express my feelings.

4. I wish I had stayed in touch with my friends.

5. I wish that I had let myself be happier.

This book is written to help you overcome these regrets and live your best life. The system I have built to develop and live your purpose will help you stay connected to what and who are most important in your life, and it will help you to be a happier person.

I started discovering and creating my purpose in 1987 and share these details in chapter one. At a crossroads in my life, my purpose was clarified. I was 26 years old and had just moved my wife and two kids across the country to enter an MBA program in the eastern part of Canada. I was one month into the program, and after getting a C minus in my economics class, I had a mini moment of crisis. The stress of the whole experience was getting to me. That weekend, I went home and wrote the first draft of my purpose statement. (I use "purpose statement" and "mission statement" interchangeably in this book). That purpose statement helped direct me to my first job and career and put me onto a path of focus, fulfillment, and ultimately, financial independence. This is discussed in more detail in the first chapter.

◊ ◊ ◊ ◊

Success literature is full of authors and ideas on how to live a fulfilling, successful, and happy life.

Which one is best and which one is right?

- Dr. Stephen R. Covey in *7 Habits of Highly Effective People* says you should develop a mission statement and plan first things first.
- Jack Canfield in his book, The *Success Principles*, says to dream big and envision success and it will be drawn to you.
- Philip Hardy, PhD, says in his book, *Personality isn't Permanent*, "After you have taken the time to really think about your future self, and about what their

circumstances and possibilities are like, your next move is to think about the one major goal or outcome that would make your future self-possible."

- Dr. Robert Maurer in his book, *Small Steps That Can Change Your Life - The Kaizen Way*, says that you should do small steps forward so as not to turn on the fear and 'fight or flight' signals in your brain.
- Dan Harris and the 10% Happier podcast team share weekly detailed meditations and podcasts about how meditation will help you to be 10% happier.

Which one of them is right? The answer is all of them. I will show you how all these ideas and concepts fit together to help you develop and live with purpose to live your best life.

There is mounting evidence and research that articulating purpose has extreme value in a person and an organizations' existence. Patrick E. McKnight and Todd B. Kashdan found that: "Devoting effort and making progress toward life goals provides a significant, renewable source of engagement and meaning. Purpose offers a testable, causal system that synthesizes outcomes including life expectancy, satisfaction, and mental and physical health." The rest of the research on benefits of purpose are found in chapter three - The Benefits of Purpose.

I commissioned my own "happiness and purpose" study of over 1,400 people to determine their habits and characteristics. The results may surprise you. Spoiler alert: The people who said they have a life purpose are 32% happier. I'll share these findings and insights throughout the book and summarize it in Section IV.

Despite the accumulated evidence, according to the McKinsey study highlighted later on in this book, only 20% of the leaders in the survey had articulated their own purpose. Why do you think that is? I believe there are four fundamental roadblocks or reasons for this:

1. People have not seen the mounting research-based evidence on the health and life benefits to living purposely.
2. They don't know how to develop or clarify purpose. A clear process has never been shared.
3. There is no clear connection and understanding on how to connect purpose with everyday activities.
4. There is a potential "shadow" side of being so focused on purpose, as there is with any strength.

This book is developed to answer these concerns and help you develop your best life.

The design principles to live your best life are:

Purpose + Plan + Practice + Acceptance + Action
= Best Life

The **Planning** practices are: Developing a purpose statement, Goal development, Weekly Planning, and Daily Planning.

The **Doing** practices are:

Deliberate and diligent practice and habits.

The **Accepting** and **Action** practices are:

Gratitude, Mindfulness, and Acceptance.

To live your best life, one must have a clear purpose, a plan to live your purpose, diligently practice living your purpose, being grateful for what does happen, accept what happened - even if it's a setback - and respond based on your purpose. It's an integrated model to live your best life and developed so you can tailor what your best life is – not your neighbors, not your parents but your best life!

The book is broken into six sections. The first section will articulate the benefits of a clear purpose and will share examples of individuals who have clear purpose. The second section is fashioned into a workbook to help you to develop, clarify, and/or sharpen your purpose. The third section will help you plan to live your purpose. It has specific recommendations to help you not lose focus on your most important roles and goals, and not to get caught up in the busyness trap. This section also gives you the planning and management system that allows you to live with purpose. In section four, we will go into what good practice looks like to accomplish goals and purpose. In section five, we review how to stay purposeful, despite stresses and setbacks that come into our lives, when we commit to an inspiring direction. Lastly, in section six, we will cover purpose at work.

At the end of each chapter, there is an application exercise to help you work out answers to questions that each chapter discusses. There is extra space to write and brainstorm ideas.

The application exercises always finish with an action plan that involves WWW – Who does What by When. Take the time after each chapter to do this internal work. I promise it will bring deeper meaning to your life.

Also included is a Lessons Learned section in most chapters. These Lessons Learned share tips and hacks to make sure each process is working for you.

I promise that if you apply the principles in this book, you will live a happier and more fulfilled life. Let's get started on developing and living your purpose.

Chapter 1

My Purpose

"The two most important days in your life is the day you are born and the day you found out why."

~ Mark Twain

This chapter is about how I found out why I was born. It explains why sharing a book about purpose is so important to me.

I was the oldest of four children growing up in Lethbridge, Alberta Canada. My parents, Dale and Renee Heyland, started me early on with goals and goal tracking. On the second cupboard by the door as you entered the kitchen, there was always a goal chart. It had my name along with all of my siblings listing chores and goals for the week for each of us. Mine had simple stuff like brushing my teeth, making my bed, reading, and playing with my little sister. I received an allowance for how many checkmarks I had on the chart. I loved that chart then and even now. I thank my parents constantly for this early start in performance management. These are my earliest memories of my love for goals, continuous improvement, and an early start for what would be my future purpose.

In my early 20s, I had heard Dr. Stephen R. Covey talk about Mission Statements as a way to articulate your purpose. I read and reread his book, *7 Habits of Highly Effective People*. Habit #2 was "Begin with the end in mind." He was big on discovering your purpose through articulating a mission (purpose) statement.

Dr. Covey was the first one that I heard say, you should envision your funeral. Imagine that you are attending your funeral. What do you want each speaker to say? Not what will they say, but what do you want them to say? It was a powerful paradigm shift. It was the first time I imagined that I could live a life based on what I wanted people to say. I remember thinking that I wanted to be respected and admired. I remember thinking I wanted people to say he worked hard and cared for people, but that is as far as I got at the time.

He also talked about a person who worked hard for years to climb a ladder, only to realize that he was very productive and efficient, but that he was going up the wrong ladder. What a huge waste to work that hard only to realize that you were in the wrong job or were not living your best life! It was a powerful motivator to figure out what I wanted to do and who I wanted to be.

Dr. Covey goes on to say the most effective way to know to "Begin with the end in mind" is to develop a personal mission statement, philosophy or creed. It focuses on what you want to be (character) and do (contributions), and about achievements and the values or principles upon which they are based. It becomes a personal constitution - the basis for making major, life-directing decisions, and the basis for making daily decisions during the circumstances and emotions that affect our lives. It empowers individuals with the same timeless strength during change.

I had not written a mission statement yet, but it got me thinking about my purpose.

A few years later, I was accepted into an MBA program in London, Ontario Canada. It was a very big decision for us to move from the west away from our family and friends and start a new adventure in the east. In 1987, my father-in-law, Ritchie Whitehead, built a small trailer for us and we drove 3,000 miles to London, Ontario. My mother-in-law, Judy, flew out later with our two oldest children so we could get the townhome set up. I remember being very intimidated on the first day of class. I was one of the younger students and the only one with kids. My work experience was not as good, varied or as long as my classmates. A majority of our grade was based on class participation. It was daunting and I felt a lot of pressure and stress. I did what I had been taught; buckle down and work hard. Very hard, maybe too hard. The cracking point came a month in. I got my first test back from our Economics class. It was one of the lowest in the class. I was now embarrassed and discouraged.

That same semester, I had also been taking a career management class. The book we were using was by Richard Bolles, *What Color Is Your Parachute*. I really liked this class and it got me thinking more introspectively. The very week I crashed in Economics class, the professor had been preaching about writing a personal mission statement. It was a beautiful fall weekend in London with crisp air and the leaves starting to change colors, but I was distraught. I was very worried I had just moved my family across the country only to fail and possibly drop out.

So, with my author/mentor Covey counseling with "Begin with the end in mind" and now Bolles repeating the recommendation about writing a mission statement, I got to work. In the middle of this mini-crisis of confidence on a Friday night after our kids went to bed, I went down to our unfinished and barely furnished townhouse basement and began constructing my mission/purpose statement. I came up with something that weekend that I continued to tweak over that semester. The process of how to develop it, I'll share later in the book. Here is what I came up with in October 1987:

My Purpose is to strive for Continuous Improvement in my life, my families', and those in my circle of influence. I want to interdependently strive for continuous improvement in my vocation, avocation, and ecclesiastical efforts.

That was it! No bells rang, no angels appeared, and my life did not change immediately. I do remember being proud of it and being at peace with the process and the work. The self-discovery involved in developing the purpose statement was extremely helpful and satisfying although it did not help me get an 'A' in Economics. The full benefits of writing this purpose statement were not evident until later the next year.

I did get better grades but there was no valedictorian speech nor were any of my classmates voting me most likely to succeed. Near the beginning of my last semester, we all found ourselves in the stressful position of trying to find *the* job. I remember interviewing for Proctor and Gamble, but did not get it and wasn't excited about that prospect anyway. I interviewed for a professor position at the local university in my hometown of Lethbridge, Alberta. I was very intrigued in the position because it did fit my interest in teaching and helping others in business management. I didn't apply for any other positions; they just didn't seem interesting.

Then came RLG International.

Their job posting said something like this: "Beyond Consulting. Join our Continuous Improvement Company and make a difference. Start working with companies where most consulting companies finished. We are looking for action-oriented people immediately to join the team."

I couldn't believe it. Some of the very words I used in the development of my purpose statement.

Continuous improvement, action-oriented, and helping others improve. Wow! I wondered if somebody had seen my purpose statement and wrote a job description! I went home and told my wife that I'd found my job and my calling. I put my resume into the job applications, and patiently or maybe not so patiently waited.

The following week, the interview list was posted, and my name was not on it! My first thought was that someone made a mistake. I called RLG headquarters in Vancouver, British Columbia, talked to one of the original partners, and told him that there was some sort of mistake. My name should have been on the list. He kindly told me that I did not have as much work experience as the other 10 candidates. I was then desperate, so I told him about my purpose statement. He told me to write my name on the list as the 11th interview at the end of the day. I was relieved. The following week, one of the partners came to the business school and patiently interviewed all 11 people. I was the only one who was moved ahead in the interview process. I was not the smartest or most qualified, but my passion and clarity came through.

My next interview was with Keith Cross, who would later be my boss and one of the great mentors I had at RLG. We met at the Toronto Airport and according to Keith, he said that I interviewed *him*! I had my Covey day planner out with a list of detailed questions about the job. In the years that followed, I was teased at company gatherings about the hiring process story, but to me, it was miraculous. It still brings a lump to my throat when I think about it. All my hard work on defining my purpose was starting to pay off. I knew what I was looking for. I went in and I got it!

I enjoyed 31 years sharing my passion for Continuous Improvement with our team and our wonderful clients and became an owner in the company. I recently retired as COO of North and South American Business. I was traveling a great deal, and knew I was getting burned out. I went back to my purpose statement to find the next steps. During this process, I was reading a book on social media that my youngest son gave to me. It was Gary Vaynerchuk's *Crush it - Why Now is the Time to Cash in on Your Passion,* and the idea came to form. I needed to start a social media brand to touch millions with the messages of Continuous Improvement and the power of purpose.

Now, semi-retired, I run an online coaching business called CI4life (Continuous Improvement 4 Life). My whole purpose is to share the continuous improvement tools and ideas I've learned over the last 30 plus years with as many people as possible.

I will share with you in the conclusion of this book my updated purpose statement. I don't believe purpose statements change substantially, but they can be tweaked as we learn and grow. I have done four formal reviews of the purpose statement since 1987 and only two revisions, but the essence remains the same.

I hope this book and my story will inspire you to find your purpose, and "find your why" that will give you more clarity and passion to live your best life. Your purpose statement will not take away stress or bad days or undesired change, but it will give you extreme focus and clarity to enjoy your life's journey. As we discuss at the end of the book, your purpose can also be a guiding force in making decisions on how to deal with financial, relationship, physical, and other types of setbacks that will occur on the way to living your best life.

Lessons Learned

Work Smart, not just Hard. We all know the value of hard work. We all need work; it gives us purpose. This Lessons Learned is about working hard and smart in the pursuit of a worthy lifelong purpose and goals. During my first semester at MBA school and right after I wrote the purpose statement, I was telling one of the professors that I was struggling and couldn't keep up with the massive reading and homework assignments that each class was giving us. He said something that has stuck with me to this day: "Work smart, not just hard." He said if you must read four large cases to get ready for four classes tomorrow, study certain parts of each case. Research it, prepare well, and participate on the section you went deep on because the classes were highly scored on class participation and debate.

That day, I learned how to work smart so I could survive and start to thrive. How does this apply to you? How can you work smarter, not harder? I think this is one of the reasons Tim Ferris's book, *The 4-Hour Work Week*, went over so well. He was teaching us how to work smart.

I love schoolteachers. I think they should be paid more for what they do. They are educating and nurturing the future of our country and our world. It is such an important job and calling. Many of them must work two or three or sometimes four jobs to provide for a growing family in our expensive economy. My brother-in-law, Mike Patterson, figured out how to work hard and work smart. He is a high school mathematics teacher and a good one. In 2009, he won both the Presidential Award for Excellence in Mathematics and Science Teaching from President Obama and the Milken Educator Award. Obtaining his undergrad in Education from the University of Alberta in 1993, he went on to the University of Georgia to earn his master's degree in Math Education in 1997. He now teaches math at the number one ranked high school in the state of Nevada. He uses a blended learning approach in math in a flexible seating classroom. It is quite progressive in that he has removed all traditional desks and chairs from the classroom and has replaced them with different seating arrangements: couches, restaurant-style booth seating, beanbags, and high-top tables and stools. He also moved all tests and worksheets from paper to an electronic format that students access with iPads.

The focus is to have students collaborate with each other and work at a pace that suits them rather than the traditional, silent classroom setting that moves too slow for the advanced students and too fast for remedial students. In 2010, Nevada adopted the Common Core standards for Geometry. He quickly realized that traditional textbooks were not going to accommodate the new standards of how geometry was going to have to be taught. He put the textbooks aside and wrote his own lesson plans, worksheets, and test bank questions. His students consistently scored top marks on district-wide exams, and he was asked to do training for the other geometry teachers in the district. From this point, he realized his materials could be used in other districts around the country and started selling them online.

Because Common Core resources were scarce, he was soon selling his materials around the country. The Department of Education in the state of Louisiana contacted him because their top geometry scores were coming from classrooms that were using his materials. They asked him to do some paperwork so he could be added to their approved list of resources. He now provides regular training to geometry teachers in Louisiana who have adopted his materials. The new need for more online teaching skills and resources has only fueled his business demand and success.

What a great example of working smart! Mike earns multiple streams of income from his primary skillset. I love the interdependence of his streams of income because as he improved his skill set and toolset for his day job, it helped with his online business and vice versa. That is following your purpose and working smart!

Application Exercise:

Let's start thinking about your purpose: How do you want to be remembered at your funeral? What do you want to hear the speakers say about you?

_____

_____

How can you start working smarter in pursuit of your purpose and goals?

_____

_____

Chapter 2

The Search for Meaning

It is a very special day!

"Everyone has his own specific vocation or mission in life; everyone must carry out a concrete assignment that demands fulfillment. Therein he cannot be replaced, nor can his life be repeated, thus, everyone's task is unique as his specific opportunity to implement it."

~Dr. Viktor E. Frankl

We all crave purpose and meaning in our lives. We all want to belong to something bigger than ourselves. You only need to look at why we belong to clubs, gangs, churches, gyms, and follow our favorite sporting teams. We need purpose and deeper meaning.

Cheryl and I have six wonderful children who are now adults and trying to live their best life. We watched each of them grow and develop in different ways with different timing. Everybody learned to walk and talk at different ages. Each one picked up different skills and abilities at different times. Some of them were great drivers the first time they got behind the wheel, and some of them acted as if they had never seen anybody drive before. To each his own!

One of the common things about them was that each of them stepped up when they found meaning and their own purpose. When they made a dance team or a basketball team, it increased and magnified their sense of responsibility and purpose. We really saw it as adults when they got married, had their first child, got their first full-time job or bought their first house. We have a running joke at our house called, "It's a very special day". We say it in a Tim the Tool Man voice. Do you remember that sitcom with Tim Taylor in the 1990s? He worked for Binford Tools and had a neighbor, Wilson, from across the fence who Tim would always share learnings with at the end of each episode, but you never actually saw Wilson's face.

Tim the Tool Man had a great voice when he was excited and he always did it when he saw a new power tool … "Hohoho" … he would say. We said it the other day when our two youngest bought their first homes. "It's a very special day when a person buys their first house – "Hohoho." Our son said it when he put in the hard work to redo his backyard. "It's a very special day when a guy builds his first backyard retaining wall or puts in his first lawn – Hohoho!" They took special pride in something they created. It was beautiful to them. We have 14 beautiful grandchildren with one more on the way as of this writing in August 2020. We have watched as each of our daughters and daughters-in-law have brought home these beautiful new babies and their lives changed forever. Yes, they have sleepless nights and difficult days, but it is an amazing thing to watch how people change when they become a parent. Their sense of maturity, responsibility, and meaning is magnified. Being a parent brings such meaning to your life!

When he was young, I could not get one of our sons to focus long enough to do his chores on time or do his homework. I had to use all of my performance management skills to encourage him to do his chores on Saturday mornings. Once he moved away from home as a 19-year-old, he found purpose, serving in Ohio for two years as a volunteer missionary in underprivileged areas. He embraced his new purpose and served with all his heart, might, mind, and strength. It was transformational to see what purpose in the service of others does to a person's life. Finding that purpose blessed his entire life as it has so many others that have done similar service efforts.

He went on to get his master's in accounting and is now CFO of his second business start-up. He and his wife are also proud parents of three wonderful kids. To be of service to others is a terrific way to find happiness and a sense of purpose. My survey of 1,400 people showed that one of the key characteristics of the happiest and most purposeful people is that they regularly serve others. I will share more details of this finding and others later in the book within the chapter on keystone habits.

I remember reading in the 1980s Viktor Frankl's book, *Man's Search for Meaning*. It inspired me to the core. Frankl was a psychologist from Austria. He was also Jewish and a prisoner in the most brutal of all camps during World War II, Auschwitz. In his book, he described the horrible situation in the camp – the dysentery and inhumane circumstances, the cold weather, the tattered clothes, the poor food. The worst of it all was not knowing if and when it was going to be your time to go into the furnaces ... your time to die. He described how many people died by choice. One way you knew when people wanted to die was when they smoked their last cigarette. The cigarette was a symbol that the individual had lost hope and the will to live. They were so exhausted and malnourished. They had lost purpose.

He also described how he survived. He survived because he had something to live for. He had purpose. He longed to see his wife again and lived for her. He also had a very specific vision for himself teaching in a warm and well-lit lecture theatre about the psychology inside the concentration camps. It was so specific how the lecture hall looked. He counseled other prisoners during the encampment and after as a psychologist and an author. He literally survived because he had very specific purposes to fulfill.

Frankl went on to be a psychological pioneer on the study of meaning. He spoke of meaning and purpose as inextricably linked phenomena, and conceived purpose as a by-product of an individual's attempt to make life meaningful. He explained that there is a "uniqueness and a singleness which distinguishes each individual and gives meaning to his existence." This "uniqueness", it has been said, is one's purpose. Frankl explained purpose as one's 'why' for living, saying that it allowed an individual to make sense of his or her circumstances (past and present), and provided them with some future goal to live for.

Indeed, it is a very special day when you find Meaning and Purpose!

Application Exercise:

What gives your life meaning and purpose?

_____
_____
_____
_____
_____
_____

What is worth living for in your life?

_____
_____
_____
_____

Is there anything that the two questions above prompts you to do to live more fully with purpose?

_____
_____
_____
_____

Chapter 3

Benefits of Purpose

"What lies behind us and what lies before us are tiny matters compared to what lies within us."

~Oliver Wendel Holmes

The top 10 benefits of living with purpose according to scientific research are:

1. Enhanced Health and Physical Well-being
2. Greater Resilience
3. Increased Happiness
4. Increased Life Satisfaction
5. Better Psychological Wellbeing
6. More likely to engage in Healthy Habits
7. Less Chronic Illness such as Stroke or Heart Problems
8. Lower Incidence of Dementia
9. Higher Quality of Life
10. Longer Life

Are you bought in? Which one of those benefits could you use more of? All of them?

Ready to start or enhance your purpose and aligned goals?

It goes without saying that the opposite is true for those who don't live a purpose-based life. They have more health problems, more psychological problems, don't live as long, and are not as happy.

In their research paper entitled, "Origins of Purpose of Life: Refining our Understanding of a Life Well Lived", Todd B. Kashdan and Patrick E. McKnight characterize purpose as:

"A central, self-organizing life aim. Central in that when present, purpose is a predominant theme of a person's identity. Self-organizing in that it provides a framework for systematic behavior patterns in everyday life. As a life aim, a purpose generates continual goals and targets for efforts to be devoted. A purpose provides a bedrock foundation that allows a person to be more resilient to obstacles, stress, and strain."

In the last 10 years, there have been several research studies done to try to quantify the benefits of having an articulated purpose. This book is sprinkled with several examples of the benefit of purpose.

Here are some of the more quantifiable studies:

This paper was published in 2014 by Eric S. Kim, Victor J. Strecher, and Carol D. Ryff and showed that there is a quantifiable improvement in health and a subsequent reduction in health care costs for those with a higher purpose:

"We found that higher purpose was linked with greater use of several preventive health care services and also fewer nights spent hospitalized. These results may facilitate the development of new strategies to increase use of preventive health care services and improve health, thereby offsetting the burden of rising health care costs in our aging society."

Here is more of the quote that I shared in the introduction of this book from McKnight and Kashdan:

"Purpose — a cognitive process that defines life goals and provides personal meaning —may help explain disparate empirical social science findings. Devoting effort and making progress toward life goals provides a significant, renewable source of engagement and meaning. Purpose offers a testable, causal system that synthesizes outcomes including life expectancy, satisfaction, and mental and physical health."

Ok. You know the research now. Why aren't more people and organizations developing purpose? Maybe they don't know how.

Application Exercise:

Which of the benefits of living purposefully could you use more of in your life?

_____

_____

_____

_____

_____

Chapter 4

The Triple 7 Process for Purpose Development

"This is the true joy in life, the being used for a purpose recognized by yourself as a mighty one."

~George Bernard Shaw

What is Purpose?

From the dictionary:

Noun: The reason for which something is done or created or for which something exists.

Verb: Have as one's intention or objective.

What Purpose is not:

It is not a list of education, experience, and skills that you have gathered in life. It is not your professional title. It is not how much money you want to make.

Purpose is the reason you were created; it is your ultimate why. A purpose statement is your life objective and intention. Dr. Stephen R. Covey's personal mission statement is a great example of a life objective and intention:

"To inspire, lift and provide tools for change and growth of individuals and organizations throughout the world to

significantly increase performance capacity in order to achieve worthwhile purposes through understanding and living principle-centered leadership."

There is no doubt in my mind that Dr. Covey's life was blessed because he lived his purpose. He also blessed millions by expressing and living his purpose. In 2002, Forbes named *The 7 Habits of Highly Effective People* one of the top 10 most influential management books ever.

Some people believe the purpose development process is a creation process (future state) and some experts believe it is a discovery process (past experiences). I say it is both. You will notice in the triple 7 process shown below is that there is a blend of future questions (e.g., what people will say at your funeral) and past questions (what are your strengths). If you're a teenager or older, you have already discovered part of your purpose, so let's start with that from the past focused questions.

Let's draw out what you know already. If we only asked past state questions, it would set you up to make a purpose that is fixed or only based on your conscious knowledge about yourself. In the future questions, you are trying to get a peek into your future self and describe and articulate that. We don't want you only working from a fixed or past mindset. In the future, you will accomplish many great and marvelous things with the experience, wisdom, and knowledge that you will possess. You are a growing and learning organism. Let's draft a purpose statement that draws from the best of your past and from the best in your future. That statement will inspire and motivate you for the rest of your life.

I promise you if you follow this process systematically, you can have a clear and compelling purpose statement that you can plan and live your future life around. This process will help you truly discover what lies within you.

If you follow the 7 questions process, it will take you 7 days and 7 hours to complete. If you do not follow this, it could take you weeks if you complete it at all. I have used this process and tested it with others. The process holds the right amount of thoughtful reflection and urgency to bring your purpose to light.

Begin with the end in mind. What does the final product look like?

The purpose statement should be a maximum of three sentences or 6 to 50 words. Anything shorter than that is a marketing slogan and anything longer than that, you might not be able to remember it and share it. You should be able to verbalize it to yourself and any one of your trusted advisors during any conversation. Previous authors have suggested that it could take months. I believe one of the reasons people do not write out their purpose is because there's not a clear process with a clear timeline. The brain needs urgency and reflection time. The reflection time is given during the 7 hours of time required to develop your purpose. The urgency is created by the 7-day clock. You can write the answers to the following questions in short bullets or full sentences - whatever works best for you.

Here is the Triple 7 Purpose Creation Process:

The process will take 7 days with 7 questions and 7 hours.

Purpose Statement Creation Process

Day 1- The Brainstorm

Answer the following questions in this book or in your favorite journal:

1. What do you want the speakers to say at your funeral? How do you want to be remembered?

_____

_____

_____

_____

_____

2. What are your strengths and why do you consider them strengths? How would your friends and family describe the best things about you?

_____

_____

_____

_____

_____

_____

3. List out the top Peak Performance events in your life. Why were they peak performance events? What did you learn about yourself?

_____

_____

_____

_____

_____

_____

4. List out the top regrets or failures in your life. What do you learn from these experiences? What will you start or stop doing because of those experiences?

_____
_____
_____
_____
_____
_____

Day 2- Reflection and Inspiration

1. Reflect on your answers from Day 1. What would you add or change to each question?

    _____
    _____
    _____

2. What have been the happiest or most satisfying experiences in your life? Why?

    _____
    _____
    _____
    _____

3. Describe your future best self? Who do you want to become?

    _____
    _____
    _____
    _____
    _____
    _____
    _____

Day 3- Making the Cut

1. Look at your lists and answers for each of the 7 questions. What themes arise? What words stand out that reflect your ideal self? Write down those summary words or short themes below.

_____

_____

_____

_____

_____

_____

2. Of the words or themes captured above, try to combine and find common themes that could go together. Finish this exercise with 3-5 key themes/words that describe your best self.

_____

_____

_____

_____

_____

_____

Day 4- Draft Day

1. Any changes from the answers from Day 3? What would you add/change or delete? (Only capture the few ideas that really represent you and your best future self.)

_____

_____

_____

_____
_____
_____

2. Write out 1-3 "draft" sentences capturing the major ideas from the words or themes in question 1 from Day 4.

_____
_____
_____
_____
_____
_____

Day 5- PS2- Purpose Statement (Rev. 2)

1. Review all your work since Day 1. Compare this review to your draft statement from Day 4. Does it capture who you really want to be? What revisions do you want to make?

_____
_____
_____
_____
_____
_____

Finish the day with PS2.

Share PS2 with two trusted advisors. Ask them for feedback after you've given them a day to think about it. Give them the evaluation criteria/questions from Day 7.

Day 6- Going Public with Limited Engagement

1. Share your PS2 with 2 trusted advisors. Ask them for feedback. Ask them if this statement captures you at your best. Review PS2 with each advisor separately.

   Feedback from TA1:

   _____
   _____
   _____
   _____
   _____
   _____

   Feedback from TA2:

   _____
   _____
   _____
   _____
   _____
   _____

2. Make any adjustments you feel necessary in PS3:

   _____
   _____
   _____
   _____
   _____
   _____

Day 7- Finals Day- Evaluation Criteria

1. Can you develop inspiring goals from PS3? If so, write down 2 of them.

   _____
   _____
   _____
   _____
   _____
   _____

2. Does the statement get you excited for the future? If so, why?

   _____
   _____
   _____
   _____
   _____
   _____

3. Does the statement tell you something you will not do or say no to?

   _____
   _____
   _____
   _____
   _____
   _____

   If you can answer yes to the above three questions, you have your final.

4. If you answered no to any questions, then look to add/subtract information so you can say yes to all 3 questions.

_____

_____

_____

_____

_____

5. Make all your final changes. Write out your Final Purpose Statement.

_____

_____

_____

_____

_____

_____

_____

_____

_____

_____

_____

_____

_____

_____

Some Examples of Purpose / Mission Statements and Insights from People Who Have Used the Triple 7 Process

Robert Mason's Purpose Statement and Analysis and Insights About the Process

1

What is your purpose statement?

TO LIVE A BOLD, EMPOWERED LIFE full of God's grace and favor that allows me to see yet to be imagined victories and cultivate that future today, through perseverance, integrity, respect, and collaboration. A future full of possibilities for myself, my family, and those around me.

2

Is it inspiring to you? Why?

Yes. It articulates well who I am as well as speaks into existence who I want to be. It recognizes God in the center of all things good now and possible in the future. I also like that it isn't all about me but aligns and brings into focus service to God, my family, and my fellow man.

3

How many words is it?

46 words.

4

How many hours and days did it take you?
It took me a couple of weeks with a coaching conversation with Rick. After the coaching conversation, it was about 2 hours.

5
What was the best question to help you?
The two questions that were most helpful in generating the input material for the purpose statement were: 1) How do friends / family see you (What do your friends and loved ones say is unique and special about you?); and 2) How do you want to be remembered by your family and friends after you're gone? (What do you want the people at your funeral to be saying about you?)

The 1:1 coaching discussion allowed me to hear how another person would package the pieces of the vision statement. Hearing this allowed me to "test" what was said and modify accordingly.

6
What was the hardest question for you?
Can you summarize your future "best self" in two sentences or less? That was a hard exercise.

7
What did you like about the process?
It was frustrating and a challenge. It did not feel natural or normal, which meant I was using parts of my brain that aren't normally engaged. It is one of the few times in life that

humility actually gets in the way of the process, so it forces you to be a more unapologetic you to get to the goal.

Nola Patterson's Purpose Statement and Analysis and Insights About the Process

1
What is your purpose statement?

I AM A CREATOR. I create beauty and happiness in my world. I am a connector. I make meaningful connections in my relationships and my physical world. I am strong. I gain strength and wisdom from my mistakes and past experiences.

2
Is it inspiring to you? Why?
It is inspiring in that just reading it makes me feel like I want to go make something. I am grateful for the ability to articulate how I feel and to see that representation on paper.

3
How many words is it?
41 words.

4
How many hours did it take you?
A little less than 7 hours. I did it in 7 days. Most days were under an hour, but I had

given some consideration to the ideas before I started this week.

5
Were you able to do it in 7 days?
If not, how many days?
Yes, in 7 days.

6
What was the best question to help you?
What have been the happiest or most satisfying experiences in your life? I liked that question because when I actually wrote my answer down, it had very little to do with what I thought my purpose statement would be.

7
What question didn't work for you?
Probably just the Day 4 assignment. The questions I found helpful. Just writing the draft was still difficult.

8
What did you like about the process?
I liked working on it each day, having time to marinate in the ideas before looking at it again the next night.

Lessons Learned

For Parents

Are your kids *your* purpose? I suggest they are only part of your purpose. What happens when they grow up, move out, and have a family of their own? Do you develop a new purpose? As we talk about this in a later chapter, no success can compensate for failing to do our best as a parent. Being a parent has such meaning and purpose, but it may not be your ultimate purpose. Your purpose is larger (but still includes your children and partner). As you answer the seven questions, you will find that larger and higher purpose of which your children can be a big part of. I know this may be a bit controversial for some, but think about it. I believe the happiest people have a bigger purpose of which their children or their spouses are a big part of. Find your bigger purpose. It could be a teacher, a servant leader, a mentor, to be creative, to be inspirational, to be bold, to teach Continuous Improvement. All of these purposes can be in service to being a great parent and spouse/partner.

Please share with me your final purpose statement and tell me how the process worked for you. My email is rickh@ci4life.org.

Congratulations! You did it! You have something to inspire you. You have a clear and compelling aspiration for your life. How exciting is that?!

Now what? How do you go about living this statement and become your best self? We will cover that in the next section.

Chapter 5

Identify Your Most Important Roles

"The first step to success is knowing your priorities."

~Aspesh

I have clarified my purpose. Now what?

In many respects, clarifying and finding your purpose is the easy part. How do I now live my purpose?

The process starts with articulating your most important roles.

We all know people that forget their purpose. Many people get so busy with their careers that they forget about their most important roles and purposes in life. Clayton Christensen wrote a terrific book about purpose. It's called, *How to Measure Your Life*. It is another high recommend.

Christensen is also a big mission statement fan for articulating his purpose. He was a Harvard Business professor. He taught and worked with the best and brightest people there. He noticed that many of the Harvard students were so singularly focused on career and success. He noticed that many would come back 25 years after graduation having achieved successful careers and earned lots of money, but now are on their second or third marriage, many of them estranged from their kids.

Professor Christensen started the ideas in this book with a talk he gave in 2010 to the graduating class of the Harvard Business School. He gave that speech with little hair as he had just started chemotherapy, the same cancer that killed his dad. The same cancer nine years later he died from. For those who attended, it was a powerful and emotional event.

Professor Christensen shared a story about a man named Steve in the book:

"Steve dreamed of owning his own business. This meant long hours at work. His family and friends understood though. After all, Steve was not doing it just because it was important to him. He was doing it for his family.

The meagerness of Steve's investments of time in his family ultimately took its toll, however. Just as his company was finally taking off, his marriage fell apart. When he needed the support of his family and friends the most, he found himself quite alone. No one intentionally deserted him in his hour of need; it was just that he had neglected them for so long that they no longer felt close to him. They worried that any intervention might be considered an intrusion.

Now he looked back over all those years and wished he'd prioritized differently - and invested in those relationships before he needed them to pay off for him.

Steve is not an isolated case. Many people are so focused on getting their careers going that they forget what is most important to them. They forget that happiness is not just about a career.

After that, Professor Christensen started teaching about purpose and mission statements to his students.

In the 1990s, there was a great version of the Peter Pan story called Hook. It starred Robin Williams, and he portrayed Peter Manning, a lawyer and successful executive who got so busy with life that he forgot his past. In the story, Peter's kids get kidnapped by Hook, a pirate portrayed by Dustin Hoffman. Tinker Bell, played by Julia Roberts, came to help Peter find his kids by remembering his past, and how important his kids were to him because he'd forgotten the people he held most dear. Eventually, with lots of coaching by Tinker Bell, Peter remembered a phrase from his past that prompts him into remembering how to "fly". As Peter Pan now, with his other helpers, they fought off Hook and saved his kids.

Envision your funeral again. What do you want them to be saying? Who do you want saying it? Yes, there will be times in your life when work or school may dominate your time, but be intentional with your roles. You'll be surprised how much you can accomplish in your other roles if you're intentional about it.

Application Exercise:

1. What are your most important roles in life?

    _____

    _____

    _____

    _____

    _____

2. What is one activity that you can do to enhance each role?

    _____

    _____

    _____

    _____

Chapter 6

Build an Integrated Life Management System to Help You Live Your Purpose

Steve's regret as articulated by Professor Christensen was that he wished he had prioritized differently. This is where goals, roles, and time management comes in. Time management will mean very little if you haven't defined your purpose. Build your purpose first and then build a management system to help you live your purpose. If you don't have a purpose clearly articulated, you're just the most efficient and productive unhappy person. Many of the very successful titans of industry in Clayton M. Christensen's book were very efficient, but they did not remember their purpose or they hadn't developed a comprehensive purpose for their whole life.

So, after you've defined your purpose, how do we build a system to help us live that purpose?

Dr. Covey's third habit was "first things first." Now that you have your purpose, we need to build in a planning system to help you not neglect the most important things that will bring you lasting happiness. That was the whole idea behind first things first. Covey talked about building a planning system that would allow you to focus on the most important or first things before the urgent things.

The Business Trap

Today, it is so easy to be busy and exhausted at the end of the day without having worked on the important meaningful and purposeful things in our lives. After 31 years of being a management consultant to successful businesses and leaders, I am still surprised how busy people are in meetings. If you look at a manager or executive's calendar today, they are so booked with meeting after meeting after meeting. This type of business life is fraught with being too busy to plan and focus on the most important things in a business or your personal life.

There are so many blessings with the internet and the information age. I could not articulate all the benefits of having automated weather, banking, news, family history genealogy, and many other things that the internet brings, but ... it does come at a cost. One of the costs is the clutter and busyness it brings to our lives. We are bombarded with news and information.

Unless you are careful, all your time will be filled before you're working on your most important things. If you're not intentional, you will get distracted. Do not let the most important people and things suffer because you got distracted.

The Problem with New Year's Resolutions

Only 25% of people actually stay committed to their resolutions after just 30 days, and only 8% accomplish them.

These New Year's goal accomplishment statistics do not inject people's confidence in the goal-setting process. There is such a stigma around it and subsequent failure for many people that they've even given up altogether on goal setting – all because their January goal setting went badly.

Goals need context and a system to accomplish them. That's why people cannot accomplish their New Year's resolutions or their yearly goals. It needs a system to support it.

It's Like a Map

Remember when we used paper maps to go on a long journey? If not, ask your parents. You had to go to the American Motor Association (AMA) and pick up a map of the states you wanted to travel. It was not even on one map usually; you had to use several maps. I remember driving in downtown Toronto for the first time with my map. I was so lost and late for my job interview. At every stop sign, I was twisting and turning that map trying to figure out where I was. I remember slamming the turn signal to turn left and doing it with such force that I broke it off ... all because of a static nonintegrated map and a frustrated "hot head" driver. We never did get that turn signal fixed on that old car. It was a constant reminder of my impatience and the importance of an integrated solution.

Today we have a fully automated GPS; the 'S' stands for system. You're able to enter your destination and the automated systems spits out the route, time required, the speed limit, and several destinations along the way. It is almost impossible to get lost. (Sometimes in new neighborhoods that aren't in the system yet, it's quite easy to confuse Google maps, but for the most part, it's reliable). The system makes your trip a reality. It is an integrated solution to help you successfully achieve your journey safely and in as little time as possible.

New Year's resolutions are like a static map. We write them on a piece of paper and chuck them in the drawer to sit for a few months until we think of it again. We pull out the paper, dust it off, and say, oh no! I was going to work on that! We need an integrated system to help us accomplish our purpose and to accomplish our goals. The system starts with effective planning.

The next planning step before we identify your most important roles and goals is to do a vision exercise. The next chapter is about visioning for personal peak experiences.

Application Exercise:

1. What are your biggest distractions?

   _____

   _____

   _____

   _____

2. What can you do to reduce those distractions?

   _____

   _____

   _____

   _____

3. What was the last goal you did not accomplish? Why? What did you learn?

   _____

   _____

   _____

   _____

4. How can you build an integrated system to help accomplish your goals?

   _____

   _____

   _____

   _____

Chapter 7

Planning for Peak Experiences

Peak experiences are events that compel us toward success and help us reach self-actualization.

Abraham Maslow describes peak experiences as such:

"The conviction that something extremely important and valuable had happened, so that the subject was to some extent transformed and strengthened even in his daily life by such experiences."

What Is Self-Actualization?

In 1943, psychologist Abraham Maslow identified the now-famous Maslow's hierarchy of needs. Maslow argued that beyond our basic needs of food, water, and shelter, our highest need is self-actualization.

Maslow describes self-actualization as, *"What a man can be, he must be."* This is the highest order of motivations which drives us to realize our true potential and achieve our ideal self. Purpose and compelling goals drive us to our true potential and our ideal self. According to Maslow, one characterization of self-actualization is having frequent **peak experiences.**

He describes a peak experience as involving:

- Feelings of limitless horizons opening up to the vision.
- The feeling of being simultaneously more powerful and also more helpless than one ever was before.
- The feeling of ecstasy and wonder and awe.
- The loss of placement in time and space.
- The conviction that something extremely important and valuable had happened, so that the subject was to some extent transformed and strengthened, even in his daily life by such experiences.

Sign me up for that! But how? How can we have frequent and intentional peak experiences?

Having a compelling purpose and compelling goals can help you have peak experiences and be self-actualized. Just ask Chris Hadfield.

Chris Hadfield is a retired astronaut and was the first Canadian Commander of the International Space Station. When Chris was nine years old, he watched Neil Armstrong and Buzz Aldrin taking the first steps on the moon. At that moment, Chris set a goal to go to the moon. Everything he did in life was focused on achieving that compelling goal.

As a teenager, Chris joined the Air Cadets. After high school, he mapped out a plan to beat the odds and become an astronaut, but at the time, Canada didn't even have a space program. Chris decided that becoming a fighter pilot and a test pilot would be the best path toward becoming an astronaut. So, against all the odds, he made the fighter pilot program and strived daily to be the best he could be.

Years later, Chris saw an ad in the paper saying that Canada was taking applications for an astronaut program. He was among thousands of applicants for two available positions. Chris went on to be the space station leader for several months in 2012, and the first Canadian to walk in space. He also sang David Bowie's, "Space Oddity" from space, which quickly went viral with over 75 million hits.

Chris's entire life was focused on a compelling goal. Interesting to note is that his dream was to walk on the moon, but people haven't been to the moon since 1972.

Was it a failure that Chris didn't accomplish his life's goal? No, because he has spent more time in space than most any other person. Look where his compelling goal made him reach and stretch to.

In 2019, I did a podcast with Chris on my Continuous Improvement 4 Life channel. Chris's life is inspiring, and he's accomplished so much because of a dream due to a compelling goal. He is an author of three books, including *An Astronaut's Guide to Life on Earth*. Chris was named the top test pilot in both the U.S. Air Force and the U.S. Navy. He was also inducted into Canada's Aviation Hall of Fame.

Chris shared a great revelation on the podcast, "We are not algae, we are not born under a rock, we are growing, learning beings that strive to become better and drive for continuous improvement toward worthy goals every day." Wow, if that doesn't jack you up, what will? Chris Hadfield knows what it is to be self-actualized because of a compelling goal. The same goes for my former neighbor, Mike Schlappi, who I interviewed.

Mike was accidentally shot by his best friend when he was 15 years old. Mike was no longer able to play the sports he was so passionate about. He lost the use of his legs, the ability to play sports, and his girlfriend due to the accident. As a teenager, Mike seemed to have lost his entire world. Mike talks about how a few months later as he was starting to settle into life in a wheelchair and then one day in the gym, he challenged his gym teacher to an arm-wrestling contest. Mike broke his arm as a result. So now he was stuck with permanent loss of his legs and the temporary loss of his arm. He only had use of one limb, which resulted in a lot of circles in his wheelchair for a few days.

One day, someone introduced Mike to wheelchair basketball, and he loved it. Playing basketball in the Olympics and representing his country soon became Mike's compelling goal.

After thousands of hours of practice and games, Mike represented Team USA in four Olympic Games playing wheelchair basketball. He won two gold medals and two bronze medals. Mike later played for and now coaches the Utah Wheelin' Jazz basketball team, who competes nationally as a member of the National Wheelchair Basketball Association (NWBA).

I've known Mike for many years now, and I've never seen him without a smile and a positive attitude about life. What impresses me more than the Olympic medals is how Mike conducts his life. He has overcome so many setbacks in life, including an unexpected divorce in between. Today, with his wife, Tami, Mike lives a fulfilling life as a speaker, Wheelin' Jazz coach, parent and grandparent, and a faithful member of the community and local church.

Mike takes his dog, Kitty, for walks almost every day with a smile on his face. When he was in the hospital as a teenager, he complained to his mom about being shot and the awful hospital food. His mom looked him in the eye and said, "Mike, don't be a crappy Schlappi, be a happy Schlappi."

His mom's advice has stuck with Mike to this day. He tells me he does have down days; everyone does. I have seen Mike accomplish three compelling goals in his life: winning four Olympic medals, building an amazing marriage with Tami (Tami has also overcome the death of her first husband to cancer and is an accomplished and compassionate person with a great attitude on life), and becoming a self-actualized Happy Schlappi!

Listen to my podcast with Mike online.

Peak experiences don't happen by accident. They need to be planned and prepared for. Chris Hadfield used his downtime to build competency and earn more certifications to be prepared for his many peak experiences. Mike took what he was given and ran (rode) with it.

If you want to read more, you can order Mike Schlappi's book, *Shot Happens,* and Chris Hadfield's book, *An Astronaut's Guide to Life on Earth,* online.

Do you want more feelings that something significant and valuable has happened so that you're transformed and strengthened? Start with this exercise.

Application Exercise:

1. What peak experiences do you want to plan for?

   _____

   _____

   _____

   _____

In the next chapter, we'll discuss how to set compelling yearly goals to accomplish more peak experiences.

Chapter 8

Goal Setting: A Step-by-Step Guide

"If you want to be happy, set a goal that commands your thoughts, liberates your energy, and inspires your hopes."
~Andrew Carnegie

How do I become self-actualized? How can I accomplish compelling goals like Chris and Mike in the previous chapter? How do I have more regular peak experiences?

In this section, I will give you a step-by-step guide to developing an effective planning system that can both help you accomplish your purpose, identify your compelling goals, and execute them in your weekly planning, all in purpose to living your best self!

Here is the 7-step Goal Accomplishment process:

1. Honor progress - not accomplishment. Start writing down all the progress you made the last year. Start your goal-setting process with a grateful, positive, and hopeful heart. More on this principle later in the chapter.
2. List your key roles. Why list roles? So you don't get so busy and forget some of your key roles. Be intentional in all areas of your life, not just work. For me, my key roles are: husband, father, grandfather, son, brother, friend, and

career. You built your list of roles at the end of chapter five.

3. Identify the categories you want to improve in. For example: financial, spiritual, emotional, work, mental/learning, and physical.

4. Develop and write SMART Goals for your roles and categories. SMART stands for Specific, Measurable, Attainable, Realistic/Relevant, and Trackable. Try to have every goal set up so you can tell if you're making progress or not. Track the lagging activity you want to improve, but also leading indicators that predict goal accomplishment. I will discuss leading indicators later in this chapter. Some examples of good SMART goals are losing 20 lbs. in 90 days, saving 10% of income or number of exercises per week - all very easy to be specific and ultimately track.

> a. An example of a SMART goal: I want to lose 20 lbs. in 90 days. It is specific; I can measure it. It is attainable and realistic because others have done it. It is also trackable. I can put my starting weight in my spreadsheet and update it each day. At the end of each week, I can see my progress and compare it to my starting point and my goal. I can then build action plans to improve.

You can do the same thing for your most important goals. For harder-to-track goals, you can try one of the following:

b. Rate it. If you have a goal to improve the unconditional love for your children, you may ask your children or your spouse how well you are doing – 1 out of 10, 10 being the highest. Perhaps you and your spouse discuss it and figure out that you're probably 5 out of 10. Then every three months, reassess and develop highlights and the next steps to improve.

c. Alternatively, you might break the goal down into measurable activities. For example, go on one date with each child per month to show interest, unconditional love, and support.

5. Build a tracking system. There are many new apps to track goals. The Strides app works well for daily tracking and provides weekly and monthly reviews. I personally still like tracking my goals in the same spreadsheet that I have used for 20+ years. It's important to be able to summarize, average, and look for trends. Have a score available to review on a daily, weekly or monthly basis, whatever is most appropriate for the goal.

6. Hold a monthly meeting. Review your averages for the month. Identify your victories and successes. Identify where you need to improve and develop plans to improve next month.

7. Share your goals with a trusted advisor. A trusted advisor is somebody that you feel safe sharing your goals with. A good, trusted advisor should give you both encouragement and a

challenge. Specifically, you should ask your advisor to give you two things: 1. Honor and acknowledge what went well. 2. Give ideas and feedback on how to improve. I recommend initially that your advisor uses the 4 to 1 ratio to help develop encouragement rather than discouragement. Give four positive encouragements to every 1 improvement idea. Build positive momentum with your goal process and your goals.

I promise if you follow this 7-step system, you'll make significant progress each month and year toward your long-term goals. You will look back on each year with deep satisfaction that you've made progress toward your best self.

Do I really have to write down my goals and track them?

Some people don't like to write down their goals. I think they believe that it might overcommit them. What if they fail? I am not that structured, they say. I just want to live chill or I just want my goals in my head. I hope to present you with overwhelming evidence that this is not the best method to help you look back on your life and say, well done, I lived my best life!

In 1992, a British psychologist set up an experiment in two of Scotland's orthopedic hospitals. The patients were on average 68 years old and had recently undergone hip or knee replacement surgeries. As many people already know, the recovery from hip or knee replacements can be very arduous and painful.

If patients don't start exercising right away, they risk blood clots and long-term restricted mobility. The pain is so extreme that many patients don't comply with their doctors' rehabilitation orders. Scientists in this experiment gave each recovery patient a booklet with blank pages and instructed them to write down their rehabilitation goals for the week, and to be as specific as possible. For example, if you had a goal to walk each day, you would write down where and why you were going to walk. The scientists then compared the recoveries of those who actually wrote in their booklets with those who didn't.

They found that those who had written goals and written plans in their booklets starting walking almost twice as fast as the ones who didn't write anything. They also started getting in and out of their chairs unassisted almost three times as fast. Another interesting finding emerged. They also recorded in their booklets how they would handle pain when it came. In other words, they wrote how they would handle setbacks to their goals.

I have dedicated Section V of this book to the challenge of responding to setbacks with gratitude, mindfulness, acceptance, and responding based on your purpose.

Starbucks, the world-wide coffee chain, is heralded as one of the most successful companies in the world. They also write specific goals and plans as part of their training for customer service. Their new employees write down how to handle certain customer service scenarios, such as, "When a customer is unhappy, my plan is to …"

Psychology professor Dr. Gail Matthews at the Dominican University in California led a study on goal setting with nearly 270 participants. The study found that you are 42 percent more likely to achieve your goals if you write them down.

Writing down your goals not only forces you to get clear on what exactly it is you want to accomplish, but doing so plays a part in motivating yourself to complete the tasks necessary for your success. The process of putting your goals down on paper will force you to ask questions about your current progress and to brainstorm your plan of improvement.

Writing down your goals and the associated plans are critical for you to live your purpose to the fullest and live your best life!

Tracking Leading Metrics is the Key to Goal Accomplishment

The key to any goal accomplishment is to break the goal down to its parts. The key question to ask is what behavior or activity would help me accomplish my goal, or what behavior predicts a successful outcome of my goal. This is the difference between leading and lagging indicators.

The lagging indicator is the result you want to achieve. The leading indicator is the predicting activity. Let me share an example to illustrate. If my goal is to increase my families' net worth this year, that is the lagging indicator or outcome I desire. The leading indicator would track the breakdown of the goal into activities that can help me accomplish the lagging results I desire.

What are two activities I can track to increase net worth? I can increase my earnings or decrease my expenses. Let's look at savings as a leading indicator. If I decrease my spending, will it help me increase my net worth? Yes. Is it a Smart indicator? Yes, it's specific, measurable, attainable, realistic or relevant, and trackable. Is it within my control to attain this goal? Can I influence this goal? Yes. I can save or reduce expenses by $1,000/month. Over the year, I can save $12k and this will improve my overall net worth. If I just focused on the lagging goal, it becomes less clear on what exactly I can do or should be doing to improve. Always break down your goals into more predicting parts. I can even break down the savings goal into more granular detail or activities. I could set a goal to spend only $20 per week on entertainment that would help me increase my overall savings which would help me improve my net worth. Think about breaking down your goals into manageable chunks. The table below illustrates other examples of lagging and leading indicators for your consideration.

Goal Category	Lagging Indicators	Leading Indicators
Physical Health	Lose 20 lbs. in the next 90 days	# of cardio workouts per week (of 30 minutes or more)
		Reduce the # of calories consumed per day
		Consume less than 100 carbs per day
Physical Health	Improve sleep by 30 minutes per night	# of nights not eating or drinking after 7 p.m.
		# of nights not using electronics in bed before sleeping
		# of meditations before bedtime per week
Physical Health	Run a 4-hour marathon	Run one interval run per week (a series of fast 1- mile runs)
		Run one long run per week (increasing 1 mile/week)

Goal Category	Lagging Indicators	Leading Indicators
		Two 5-mile runs per week
Financial Security	Increase net worth	$ earned per month
		$ saved per month
		$ saved on entertainment (or any other category)
Financial Security	Earn 33% in the stock market	Adjust portfolio at opening bell each day
		Adjust portfolio at closing bell each day
		Number of financial newsletters read each day
		Watch CNBC business news daily for 30 minutes

I could go on, but you get the idea. Any goal can and should be broken down into its most controllable parts. You should identify the exact activities to track to accomplish your lagging goals. All of the leading indicators should be activities within your control that are measurable and very specific. These leading indicators are SMART.

The same thing can be done with work goals. Let me share a few to get you started on your own leading and lagging indicators.

Goal Category	Lagging Indicators	Leading Indicators
Sales	Increase sales by 10%	Read a sales training book every month
		One lunch with a sales expert per week
		# of client calls per week
Safety	Reduce recordable injuries by 12%	# of safety observations by the front-line per week
		# of safety observations by management per week
		# of effective safety meetings per week

Goal Category	Lagging Indicators	Leading Indicators
Morale	Improve job morale (as measured by an employee survey)	# of community events per month
		# of effective and empowering employee meetings per month
		# of employee ideas followed up on
		# of recognition awards per month

The key is finding the right leading indicator that actually influences the lagging outcome that you are trying to improve. You can waste a lot of time and effort by not tracking the right leading indicator. Or alternatively, you cannot hit your lagging goals by missing a key leading indicator. Quality of activity is also a huge influence on your success.

Let me share some examples.

Key goal - Run a marathon at under 4 hours. If you don't have a leading indicator for an "interval run" (fast-mile training day), you will not build the speed fast enough to accomplish your 4-hr. target.

Key goal - Improve Safety. If you don't track the number of front-line observations or engagements that the front-line are doing, you will not engage them enough to become part of the result you are looking for. Also, if your safety meetings are not engaging enough or high quality, they can actually become a deterrent to improving safety.

Plan small next steps for your goals.

As Dr. Bob Maurer says in his book, *Small Things That Change Your Life - The Kaizen Way*, he describes a breakthrough he had while working at a hospital. Dr. Maurer learned that taking small steps led to the task being done and then his patients were able to work toward goals that were more ambitious.

One example highlighted in his book is a patient who came in several times with high stress, weight gain, and unhealthy habits. The doctors previously recommended the patient start at losing 20 pounds, but she was not able to get started. When Dr. Maurer asked her if she watched T.V. when the kids went to bed at night, she said yes. Dr. Maurer asked if she could do jumping jacks during one commercial break at night, and she said she would.

She came back the next week and reported success with the small task. As the weeks went by, Dr.

Maurer asked her to do jumping jacks during all of the commercial breaks and steadily increased the amount of exercise. In six months, she reached her goal of losing 20 pounds.

Dr. Maurer learned this technique from Japanese Kaizen. Kaizen is a Japanese continuous improvement technique that trains employees to find small faults in their factories to continually improve. Dr. Maurer talks about how the limbic system is fired up with fear when talking about big, daunting goals. However, it stays quiet if you start with small goals. I highly recommend the book. If you want just a 30-minute version, please listen to my podcast with Dr. Maurer.

Dream big. Have goals to self-actualize and then identify small steps and leading indicators to start progressing. Don't overwhelm yourself. The key is identifying small steps and leading indicators.

Honor progress, not just accomplishments of your goal. This may be one of the most important personal and organizational lessons for goal accomplishment. It is such an important motivational strategy! Yes, go ahead and set or stretch aspirational targets for yourself and/or for your team, but make sure and honor progress, not accomplishment. Ken Blanchard, the author of *The One Minute Manager* and many other good books, used to teach the 'training a whale' example to illustrate this point. The trainers don't go out in the middle of the ocean and yell into a megaphone. Any whale that can jump over this rope will receive a great reward of all-you-can-eat fish. They start the rope underwater and every time the dolphin, seal or whale goes over the rope, they get a fish treat. The trainers know that the ultimate stretch target is to jump over the rope high in the air and land with a big splash. However, they start low and honor progress - every time raising the rope a bit higher until they get to the goal.

Strategic Coach founder Dan Sullivan says it this way: "Measure back from where we are currently to where we started, and we're rewarded by all the progress we've made. We feel happy and satisfied about how things are going, and our confidence takes an immediate leap. This is what I call *The Gain*."

Too many people wait until they achieve their ultimate weight loss goal, for example, until they reward themselves with a pat on the back or a new pair of shoes. The real motivational strategy for recognition is to honor progress and gain. It is so simple, yet so powerful. Yes, I have not achieved my goal of losing 20 pounds, but I have lost 5 pounds and that is progress. I had a goal to exercise 5 times last week, but I exercised 4 times. Is that a failure? No, because my baseline (history) was 3 times per week. Honoring progress versus accomplish is a huge mental motivational edge for your goal accomplishment success.

Atomic Habits author James Clear says it this way: "You should be more concerned with your current directory than your current results. If you are a millionaire but you spend more than you earn each month, then you're on a bad trajectory. If your spending habits don't change, it's not going to end well. Conversely, if you're broke, but you save a little bit every month, then you're on a path toward financial freedom - even if you're moving slower than you'd like."

James Clear continues: "Breakthrough moments are often the result of many previous actions, which build up the potential required to unleash a major change. This pattern shows up everywhere. Bamboo can barely be seen for the first five years as it builds extensive root systems underground before exploding ninety feet into the air within six weeks."

Focus on the small victories every day - that is what leads to great lagging results. This principle captures the essence of proper goal accomplishment. Be grateful and give recognition to small steps forward because it's leading to great accomplishments.

If I put my organizational hat on, I will tell you this is one of the most under-utilized motivational skills in corporations today. As leaders, we are good at setting compelling and aspirational goals, but generally we don't "honor progress". It is soul-destroying to the individual and the team. Many leaders still don't honor progress - just the result. They lose a powerful motivational tool to help them accomplish their goals.

As you follow this 7-step goal accomplishment process and the principles I have outlined, you will have success in accomplishing many peak experiences.

Lessons Learned

Goal Setting #1

People love to be around people who are interested in others. Don't be so consumed with your personal goals that you're not focused on people and relationships. It can be very powerful and intoxicating to be eating healthy or training for a marathon, for example. These are very exciting goals, but they are your goals. Have you ever been around somebody on a special diet that is changing their life? It's all they want to talk about. How about when you're training for a marathon? It's all life-consuming in a very good way. It changes the way you eat, sleep, exercise, and plan your day. Just remember to show interest in what others are doing. Nobody wants to be around somebody who only talks about their own passions. My oldest son recounted a story about his younger sister. He said, "We had a 30-minute conversation to catch-up the other day. I realized when I hung up that she had been so skillful with her questions and her interest in me that we talked all about my stuff and I really didn't find out how she was doing."

His sister had some very interesting things going on in her life, but she was genuinely curious and interested in what was going on in her older brother's life. People are drawn to people who show genuine interest in others. What a great life skill!

Lessons Learned

Goal Setting #2

Going public with your goals. Public commitment is a big part of the goal-setting process. You do not have to share it with strangers. Initially, make your goal declarations with trusted advisors. However, there is huge value in making a public declaration. It makes your commitment stronger. I showed interest in writing a book for over 30 years but was never committed. It wasn't until I read Chandler Bolt's book called *Published - The Proven Path from Blank Page to Published Author* that I actually committed. The first thing I did was to share with several of my family members and closest friends that I was going to write a book. It was a bit scary, but it forced me to stay committed to my goal. I asked my family and friends to ask me how I was doing every time they saw me. This kept me very committed. Do the same thing with your financial goals, with your exercise goals, with your nutrition goals, etc.

Lessons Learned

Goal Setting #3

Start small - don't overwhelm yourself. If the whole goal-setting system grabs your limbic system and freezes you from action, have no fear. Start small. Start simple. Start with one goal. Gain confidence with the system and then add more goals later.

The 3 main areas in one's life are usually: (1) Financial security and/or Independence; (2) Relationships; and (3) Health and Wellbeing. Start with one goal and a leading indicator, track it, review it, and gain confidence as you learn and progress toward your purpose and best self.

Lessons Learned

Goal Setting #4

Use your strengths for goal accomplishment. If you are a relationship person, use your strength to help accomplish your goals. Invite family and friends to join you in accountability for or actually joining in the goal. My wife, Cheryl, is a people person. She regularly exercises with friends and exercises for sociality. She uses her strength to keep her motivated and interested in exercise. I am more of a task-oriented individual (as if you couldn't guess that from reading this book!). I love goal accomplishments. For more relational-type goals, I set goals (prioritized weekly and daily plans/tasks) to accomplish them. For example, I set a goal each week to connect with my parents and children. If I write it down as part of my weekly plan, it has a high probability of happening. I guess the critic could argue that I should just do those things naturally. I would make the argument that in our busy lives, important things need to be planned and prioritized so we can put our best thinking toward such important goals. Use the strengths that you have developed to your benefit.

I hope this section has helped you think about your strengths and how you can use those strengths for goal accomplishment. You can accomplish any goal if you tap into your strengths!

Application Exercise:

1. What are some of the SMART goals you want to improve on?

    _____
    _____
    _____
    _____

2. What are your leading indicators for those goals? How will you track your progress?

    _____
    _____
    _____
    _____

3. Who will be your trusted advisor that you can share your goals and plans with?

    _____
    _____
    _____
    _____

Now, we need to integrate your purpose and yearly goals into a weekly planning process.

Chapter 9

Weekly Planning as a Superpower

The time you spend weekly planning could be the most important 30 minutes of your week!

Dallin H. Oaks, former Utah Supreme Court Justice said:

"We should begin by recognizing the reality that just because something is good is not a sufficient reason for doing it. The number of good things we can do far exceeds the time available to accomplish them. Some things are better than good, and these are the things that should command priority attention in our lives."

Have you ever felt like the day just flew by?

Perhaps you were tired or overwhelmed. Every minute seemed to be full. Days like this can feel fulfilling at the end of the day, but be careful.

Ask yourself, how many of those activities were empty calories? Alternatively, how many were good calories but not the best calories?

Do not let good activities rob you of great activities. When you look back on those busy days, how many of your goals did you accomplish?

The need to be busy is one of the worst addictions of our time.

As I mentioned in the introduction of this book, one of the biggest regrets people have when they're dying is that they worked too hard and didn't pay enough attention to their central relationships. The other common regret is that they didn't live their best life.

One reason people don't live out their purpose or reach their long-term goals is that they do not have a system to match their bigger purpose with their day-to-day activities. Most people have trouble staying focused on their most important tasks and relationships.

The busyness and distractions of the modern-day world are powerful and plentiful. The constant call for meetings and never-ending notifications on your phone are tough to ignore.

In addition, marketing professionals and advertisers are getting more and more sophisticated. They are listening and sending you the ads that you're interested in. These calls to action are also difficult to ignore.

So, what do you do?

Weekly planning is a terrific way to stay focused on your purpose and the important relationships and activities in your life. Planning your week is an opportunity to be intentional and get rid of the time wasters – or even some of the good-but-not-great activities throughout our day.

Weekly Planning is a Superpower

Develop your weekly plan during a commercial-free, interruption-free, and notification-free period. This is the most important 30 minutes of your week. Treat it as such.

Build in times during the week that you can go notification-free so you can focus on your number one activities. Hide your phone, turn off notifications on your computer, and focus your mind on the most crucial task. You will feel an increased clarity and focus on what's at hand.

I recommend investing in a **weekly planning system (found on www.ci4life.org)** to help you organize time around your purpose, roles, and goals. Doing so also helps you prioritize.

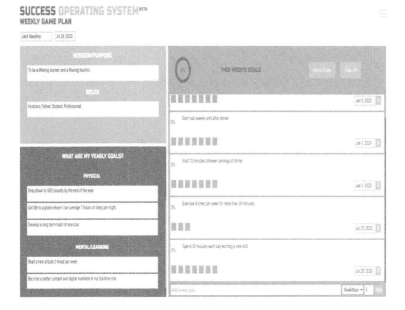

As you can see in the weekly game plan above, your purpose, roles, and goals are along the weekly game plan's left-hand side. These remain mostly static during the year. Each week, you will identify the weekly activities that help you accomplish the goals you have identified. You must find a consistent time every week to plan. Consistency trains your brain to be prepared and ready for a productive planning session.

Here are seven steps (4 + 3) you can walk through for your weekly planning session.

4-Step Weekly Planning Session

1. **Schedule your weekly planning session** the same day and same time each week. For example, 7:00 p.m. each Sunday.
2. **Review the past week**. Start with reviewing the highlights of your week. What were you most proud of? What were your big successes? What did you learn from, setbacks or wins? How can you apply what you learned this week?

   For example, let's say you planned your reading/studying time during the evening, and you had four interruptions during the evening that prevented you from reading. Those interruptions came from important family and friends. What could you do differently to accomplish your goals? Perhaps you could do the reading another time. This week you can try switching your time to when there are fewer interruptions.

3. **Plan your most important activities**. Look at your purpose, roles, and key goals and plan your key activities for the week. Plan the important non-urgent things. I never include scheduled meetings that are in my calendar unless they need a big planning component. If you include all of the urgent/planned things, you will overwhelm yourself. Plan to have 10-20 important non-urgent activities each week that are small steps toward your big goals.

4. **Schedule your weekly activities**. Try to schedule your 10-20 important items into your week. Use your calendar to plan these activities. For example, if you want to start 30 minutes of aerobic exercises five days a week, calendar it in at 6.30 a.m. every weekday.

Follow up throughout your week with daily planning. Each day as you plan, look at your weekly plan. You should complete a 3-step process for your daily plan.

3-Step Daily Planning Session

1. **Put a checkmark next to the completed items.** Have a mini-celebration in your head for every activity you completed. Celebrating your wins gets some positive endorphins going inside.

2. **Check and see which weekly planning items are already planned.** Mentally prepare for those important activities.
3. **Add items that were either not scheduled or must be rescheduled** because they were not accomplished earlier in the week.

Other Tips for Weekly Planning

To develop this productivity superpower, you need to:

- Plan during the same time each week and day. Train your brain to recognize the event and the time and you will enhance your planning effectiveness and efficiency.
- Find a place in your house for planning. Train your brain that this is the planning space. You can train your brain to recognize the time and place, and it will respond with increased concentration and efficiency.
- Put your most important activities during quiet times—the times when you will get the least interruptions. Don't be afraid to update your calendar in the morning or at lunch to include key non-urgent activities in your weekly plan.
- Plan activities with those who are most important to you. I am still surprised after 40 years of using this planning system how many "highlights of the week" come from relationship activities. For example, a good talk with my wife during our Saturday morning run always makes my weekly gratitude list. Exercise and

connecting with your spouse are a double endorphin hit!

Lessons Learned

You are about to develop a motivation and productivity superpower. Be careful with your kryptonite.

1. **Be intentional but flexible**. Little kids are the classic example of this. Kids do not understand weekly and daily plans. Of course, you can coach them to honor your time, but you must be flexible and open to making changes. People are more important than tasks or efficiency.

2. **Because you are a super planner, your time is not more important than others**. Remember what and who is most important in your life. As you follow this plan, you will become more focused, motivated, and productive. Close members of your family will see the pros and cons of this.

   Just the other day, my youngest daughter reminded me that my time was not more important than hers. I was asking her to do a task around the house so I didn't have to worry about it, and then I could focus on writing this chapter in my book. "Dad, I am working on my important tasks." She was doing her homework. "It sounds like you're saying your time is more important than mine." I quickly apologized and thanked her for giving me honest feedback.

3. **Customers first!** If you run a small business, you know that things can get very busy. There are many hats to wear all at once. You are the problem-solver for many employee and customer issues. For a small business, serving and caring for the customer is the life blood of your business. I know many business owners who get so busy with "running the business" that they don't interact with the people who are paying for their services. In many small businesses, there is very little customer/client interaction. I think this is a classic example of letting the urgent distract us from what is most important. Linda Schiele at the local PostNet in Draper, Utah understands this principle. She is a typical busy small-business entrepreneur, but when you walk into her shop, you think you're the most important person in the world. She greets everybody with energy, enthusiasm, and interest. Whether you are a local print and post services shop, a consulting service, a local lawn maintenance company, a dentist's office or a rental company for

medical equipment, remember what and who is most important in your week. Because entrepreneurs can get so busy fixing and building stuff, I recommend they set a goal, a weekly plan, and track significant client/customer interactions.

4. **Personal Check-ins.** Plan check-ins with your loved ones or key employees. Don't have a planned agenda. Just check in to see how they are doing. Don't assign an action item. Just listen and find out how they are doing. Rick Mazur, one of the original partners in RLG International, was the best at this. He would take you on a walk and say, "How is Rick Heyland doing?" He built tremendous loyalty because it showed he cared.

Do not let busyness rob you from doing what is most important in your life. Don't get sucked into the exhausting and empty calories that busyness can bring. Focus on what is most important in your life and then plan around it. A good weekly planning system can help you live with no regrets and live your best self!

Chapter 10

Daily Planning
The Most Important Daily Habit

There's a good argument to be said that regular exercise is the most important habit. Charles Duhigg, author of *The Power of Habit,* calls exercise the keystone habit.

I agree that exercise is a keystone habit that leads to a better life. Even for a few minutes every day, a habit of exercise is a guaranteed way to become healthier and happier.

On a similar note, people might argue that the most important habit is hard work. James Cash Penney, better known as the founder of JCPenney, once said:

"Unless you are willing to drench yourself in your work beyond the capacity of the average man, you are just not cut out for positions at the top."

No doubt, being diligent and hardworking is a crucial attribute for success and happiness.

The most important habit: Planning your day

I would argue that making a plan; specifically, a daily plan, is the most important habit.

In my survey of over 1,400 people, one of the things I wanted to determine is to find out the characteristics of the most happy and purposeful people. The results showed that 70% of those who said they had above-average happiness said they had a habit of daily planning. That was more than double of those who reported below-average happiness. Of those who reported having a life purpose, they practiced daily planning 20% more than those without a life purpose. Daily planning is the most important habit.

High Performance Habits author Brendon Burchard's research agrees: "High performers plan almost everything more than underperformers do; from work-outs to learning, from meetings to vacation time. Know the big five moves that will take you to your goal, break those down into tasks and deadlines, then put them into a calendar. If that's all you did – and make sure you made these moves aligned with your purpose – you'd be ahead of the game."

I have found that 15 minutes in the morning and evening to plan and review sets up all other daily habits. It's during the quiet planning time of the morning and evening that you plan your exercise, work, and all your other good and worthwhile activities of the day.

Ancient philosophers, known as Stoics, emphasized the importance of morning planning. Roman emperor Marcus Aurelius suggested to remind yourself in the morning "of what a precious privilege it is to be alive – to breathe, to think, to enjoy, to love."

Epictetus advised to rehearse the day in the morning and then review your progress in the evening. At daybreak, we should ask ourselves a few questions:

- What do I still lack in order to achieve freedom from negative emotions?
- What do I need to achieve tranquility?

I found that a morning planning meeting with myself can turbo-boost my day. When you get off to a good start, the rest of the day will follow suit.

Waking up early to conduct your morning planning is essential because it's quiet, and you can be still and free from interruptions. Early mornings are a time where you can connect to your soul and listen without worrying about the business of life.

What should my morning planning meeting look like?

1. **Start with gratitude**. Use your phone or a journal to list the things you are grateful for in that moment and yesterday. This is a great way to start your day with positivity!
2. **Build your daily plan after looking at your weekly plan and then calendar it**. After looking at your weekly plan, build it. Write your plan in the order that you want to accomplish it. A good daily plan helps visualize the activities and helps with last-minute planning for each activity. If your daily plan has 20+ items on it, prioritize your top three activities based on importance. Put a star beside them so when the reactivity of the day starts and there are unscheduled break-

ins happening, you can always go back and calendarize and prioritize the big three.

3. **Mentally prepare for how you want to show up**. Build an intention for the day. How do you want to show up for your spouse/partner and kids? How do you want to show up under challenging decisions or issues at work? A morning meditation practice is a great way to prepare for the day.

4. **After your planning session, start your renewal activities**. Build your emotional and physical capacity by planning and completing your exercise and spiritual practices. There are so many positive endorphins from morning exercise. Research shows that after exercising, you are highly productive for the next few hours. The spiritual/emotional activities after the planning session increase your emotional capacity. This is a time to set an intention for the day. Yoga, meditation, prayer, and scripture study are terrific habits to practice in the morning.

What should my evening review look like?

1. **Start building your gratitude list for the day**. Gratitude allows you to not focus on the one thing that went wrong and train the brain to focus on what went right. The other day I had 18 things to do on a Sunday. I accomplished 17 things and did not accomplish my last goal of not eating sugar after 8 p.m. As I sat down for evening planning and preparation, I found myself focused on the one thing that went wrong. Has that ever happened to you? After my gratitude exercise, my mind started to focus on

the 17 things I accomplished. The evening went so much better when I focused on what went right.

2. **Review what you learned**. What did I learn today? What did I do well today? What can I do better? Write the answers to these questions down. I love thinking about what I learned each day. Many of my blog posts and podcasts come from my daily learnings.

3. **Practice acceptance**. Acceptance of reality is a key that unlocks happiness. You can plan your whole day, but usually it won't go exactly how you planned. Expressing gratitude for what went well and accepting what did not go as planned is an attitude that leads to happiness. You will face success and blessings along with disappointments and discouragement. We need to accept it all! I found a thoughtful article on acceptance from a psychotherapist and wellness writer, Megan Bruneau.

Here is an excerpt:

"No one is suggesting you like, want, or support whatever it is that you're accepting. However, by struggling against the pain—by resisting and rejecting it—we create undue suffering. It does not mean that you have chosen or endorse what you are accepting. It does not mean you like your anxiety, want your chronic pain, would choose your body or support an injustice that has happened to you or someone else. Rather, you are choosing to allow it to be there when you cannot change it in that moment. To make space for it. To give yourself permission to be as you are, feel what you feel or have experienced what you have experienced without creating unproductive shame or anxiety. The pain might still be there, but some of the suffering will be alleviated." I will have much more on the practice of acceptance in a later chapter.

4. **Start your daily plan for tomorrow**. Get a head start on tomorrow's plan. Carry over the items that were not done from today. Remember to always start with the same physical, spiritual, and emotional practices right after your morning planning session.

5. **Finish your daily review with a short meditation session** to relax your mind and prepare for sleep.

Performing these daily practices will help you to look forward to the sessions to reflect and learn. You will find an enormous amount of joy from checking off the items on your daily plan. I am slightly embarrassed to admit how much I love checking things off my daily plan.

When you build and maintain the discipline to plan every morning and every evening, you will accomplish your wildest dreams and aspirations. Systematically, you'll be creating a practice of progress that becomes very self-reinforcing.

Lessons Learned

Daily Planning #1: It's not a to-do list or a checklist. There is a big difference between a randomly ordered to-do list and a prioritized daily plan. The daily plan is based off of your most important activities and time blocked to maximize the effectiveness of those relationships and activities that are most important to you.

Daily Planning #2: Remember to be patient with yourself, with others, and issues that throw off your plan. Relationships always take precedence over tasks. Be intentional in building relationships and connections as part of your daily plan!

Daily Planning #3: Planned Flexibility. Don't over-plan. Don't plan every 15 minutes. Leave time for important break-ins in your day. My wife has successfully raised six kids with a husband who travels a few days per week for over 30 years. Part of her magic is to have a plan when she starts the day but to always be flexible if a higher priority comes up. She generally has several projects to work on for her service activities, crafts or house projects. If a child or good friend comes up with a break-in that is important, she quickly pivots from a planned project. These, of course, are possible if you do not have a hard deadline.

Daily Planning #4: Set three alarms. As you can tell from this book, I like 'life hack' ideas. A life hack is a trick, strategy or technique adopted in order to manage one's time and daily activities in a more efficient and effective way. Eric Partaker is coming out with a book called, *The Three Alarms*. He is a business coach in Europe and was recently chosen as CEO of the year. I heard him recently on the SPI podcast with Pat Flynn (a high recommend for entrepreneurs). As a fairly young father and successful Skype executive, he experienced a life-changing event that got him thinking about designing and planning sustainable effectiveness into his life. He suffered a heart attack on a flight. After recovery, he dedicated his life's work to figuring how to build sustainable practices of personal and corporate development. His hack is to set three alarms in your phone with a list of routines so that you have daily reminders for your daily habits. This helps ensure a more successful completion of your most important daily activities and habits.

Try these four alarms: (1) 9 p.m. - Prepare for sleep and plan tomorrow; (2) 6.30 a.m. - Plan for the day; (3) 6.45 a.m. - List your renewal activities such as exercise and other mental and spiritual developmental routines; and (4) 8.30 a.m. - Crush the day!

Daily Planning #5: Plan in renewal activities. Please remember to plan in "downtime" to relax and enjoy life with friends and family. You will be more successful in the long run if you're not working 100-hour work weeks. This is not a sustainable life practice. The goal is to have 85 years of a happy purposeful life – not to burn out in 20 years. If you build in renewal time, you will make better business decisions. Your mind will be clearer and sharper. You will respond to setbacks better if you have taken time to have fun and relax.

It is an incredible feeling of productivity and success to be a good daily planner. I believe that daily planning is the most important habit for sustainable happiness and purposeful living.

Application Exercise:

1. What do you currently do for daily planning?

   _____

   _____

   _____

   _____

2. What ideas would you like to implement from this chapter to enhance your happiness, purposefulness, and productivity?

   _____

   _____

   _____

   _____

3. Develop an Action Plan from question 2: 'Who' does 'What' by 'When'.

   _____

   _____

   _____

   _____

Chapter 11

Practicing and Doing on Purpose

"With the right kind of diligent practice, you can enhance any skill or ability."

~Rick Heyland

How did the greats accomplish their goals? How did the best athletes and the best musicians become great? How did the captains of industry become the best? Were these individuals just born with their abilities? Did they come out of the womb as the smartest, the most inclined, the most capable?

No! Regardless of innate ability or circumstance, every individual who can claim any real success had to work for it and practice. If you're trying to develop a new gratitude, meditation or acceptance skill, it will take dedicated practice for you to master the techniques. If you're trying to become a master investor, it will take dedicated and deliberate practice. Many people give up on their goals after trying for a little bit saying, I am just not cut out for that or it does not work.

Most masters of any domain meet two criteria:

1. They had expert teachers
2. They practiced more than others did.

These two ingredients make up the recipe for being the best you can be.

Practice Outpaces Talent

Consider Jerry Rice. Jerry is the greatest American football receiver of all time. Was it because he was the fastest or the best jumper? Nope! He was not either. He was, however, the best at practicing. Rice worked out six times a week in the off-season. He practiced the skills necessary to become a great receiver. He practiced much more than he played.

Consider Jack Welch. Jack was recognized as the leader of the century during his reign over GE. He was often quoted as saying, "No one would mistake me for a genius," but he was able to find a mistake or opportunity in an income statement faster than anyone.

How did he do it? Did he have a specialized education? Yes, but in chemical engineering. Few would doubt that he was a sharp man, but what was it that made it possible for him to become so exceptionally nimble in his domain? The short answer: practice and dedicated learning.

Talent Is Overrated

Geoff Colvin writes a terrific book titled, *Talent Is Overrated*. In his book, Colvin asserts that deliberate practice is what makes excellent performers. One particularly salient example from his book is of Laszlo Polgar.

Laszlo Polgar lived in the 1960s and was a Hungarian educational psychologist. Polgar was certain that great performers were made, not born. In accordance with his belief, he advertised for someone to marry him, stating that together they would raise children from a young age to be world-class chess players. His soon-to-be wife Klara accepted the proposal, and the two of them raised three daughters (Susan, Sophia, and Judit) to become chess grandmasters.

How did Laszlo and Klara get their three-peat? Through deliberate practice from a young age. Laszlo didn't know anything about chess until the children began to grow, but he made up for lost time. The family was said to have 10,000 books on chess in their library. When Susan was 19, Sophia, 14, and Judit, 12, they competed as a team in the Women's Chess Olympiad and scored Hungary's first ever victory against the Soviets, becoming national heroes.

The learnings from Laszlo Polgar for personal and professional continuous improvement are plentiful and hopeful.

To become a great golfer or runner or cyclist takes a lot of deliberate practice. Think back on Jerry Rice, who practiced more than he played. Couldn't you try that with your golf game — practice more and play less? Learn the skills and right drills to become great.

Bring Purposeful Practice to your goals

Let's say one of your work goals is to have excellent meetings that motivate and engage your team and vault them on to weekly success. Do you prepare so they can become great?

Take a second to gauge the successfulness of your current meetings. What would you score your weekly meetings at out of 10? If you are 5 out of 10, what should you do to score a 10? Here is the formula based on the lessons of purposeful and deliberate practice.

1. Identify what a great meeting looks like. Have experts help you identify best in class.
2. Share and agree on that expectation with your team.
3. Measure your success versus the ideal.
4. Get feedback from a meeting expert and your team.
5. Course correct and adjust to become a 10.

You can see how this can apply to any skill or discipline. Do you want to become a great financial investor? Apply the following steps:

1. Identify what a great financial investor does.
2. Commit to practicing great financial learning and acumen every day.
3. Measure yourself versus your commitment.
4. Adjust and course correct with a trusted partner, creating some joint accountability.

Warren Buffet's story can shed some light on how experience and practice can open the path to becoming a great investor:

"[Warren Buffet] purchased his first stock when he was 11 years old and worked in his family's grocery store in Omaha. His father, Howard Buffett, owned a small brokerage, and Warren would spend his days watching what investors were doing and listening to what they said. As a teenager, he took odd jobs, from washing cars to delivering newspapers, using his savings to purchase several pinball machines that he placed in local businesses."

Buffet then went on to complete a business degree before applying for additional graduate studies:

"After being rejected by the Harvard Business School, he enrolled in graduate studies at Columbia Business School. While there, he studied under Benjamin Graham – who became a lifelong friend – and David Dodd, both well-known securities analysts. It was through Graham's class in securities analysis that Buffett learned the fundamentals of value investing. He once stated in an interview that Graham's book, The Intelligent Investor, had changed his life and set him on the path of professional analysis to the investment markets. Along with Security Analysis, co-written by Graham and Dodd, it provided him the proper intellectual framework and a road map for investing."

Was Warren Buffet born with an insight to business or did he learn it from experts and then put hours and hours into studying charts and businesses? I suggest the latter. Mr. Buffett is now into his 80's and still shows up for work every day.

Good Practice Makes Perfect

Receiving coaching from an expert is critical if you want to become the best you can be. Tiger Woods had many coaches, starting with his dad, then many others followed.

Which exposes an important point: Fathers and mothers can instill in their children the importance of practice and (should) be their first teachers. Tiger Woods' first coach was his dad. Warren Buffet's first mentor was his father, the stockbroker. Beethoven's father was a master teacher.

Find Someone to Direct Your Practice

Regardless of the relationship or the age of the student, finding the right teacher is essential.

In his best-selling book, *Talent is Overrated*, Geoff Colvin believes in this principle:

"Anyone who thinks they've outgrown the benefit of a teacher's help should at least question that view. There's a reason why the world's best golfers still go to teachers.

"One of those reasons goes beyond the teacher's knowledge. It is his or her ability to see you in ways that you cannot see yourself.

"It's apparent why becoming significantly good at almost anything is extremely difficult without the help of a teacher or coach, at least in the beginning. Without a clear, unbiased view of the subject's performance, choosing the best practice activity will be impossible; for reasons that may be simply physical (as in sports) or deeply

psychological, very few of us can make a clear, honest assessment of our own performance."

As Colvin explains, we need teachers and coaches to give an outside perspective of ourselves. So, if you want to create a step change in any skill or practice:

1. Hire a coach or expert to help you identify what "great" looks like.
2. Practice those newfound skills with quality and excellence.
3. Continue to adjust and modify based on the coach/expert's feedback.
4. Experience a "step change" in your skill and abilities.
5. Repeat.

You do not have to be a "natural" to accomplish your goals and dreams. Just be willing to accept coaching from experts and then implement lots of deliberate practice to increase your skills and abilities in order to meet your goals and live your purpose.

I have heard too many people say they aren't good at math or "I can't sing" or "I am not good at sports" or "I am not good with money". That is not a learner's mindset. All skills are absolutely doable and learnable. You may not be the next LeBron James or the next Taylor Swift, but you can accomplish and develop any skill with the right practice.

Lessons Learned

For Purposeful Practice

Become a student of the game! Have you ever heard that saying before? They say it about Lebron James, the famous basketball player for the Los Angeles Lakers. Basketball experts talk about how Lebron works hard and studies the game. He studies the habits and practices of the past greats. He learns everything about health, fitness, and mental training techniques so he can be his best.

Nate Goodfellow is a sales rep with Candlewarmers Inc. Candlewarmers is my oldest son's company that he owns with his brothers-in-law based out of Draper, Utah. On a sales trip, Nate's buddy told him one night that he was overweight. Nate at first denied the feedback, but later realized it was true. He went on a wonderful journey for the next several years on how to get back in shape and became a student of his chosen goals. He has lost 50 pounds and has kept it off for years. He did it through reading and talking to experts about exercise and nutrition. Nate became obsessed with learning and practicing the right skills, habits, and activities of health and fitness.

You can hear his entire story on my podcast at: ci4life.podbean.com.

Become a student of your game! Become obsessed with Diligent Practice!

Application Exercise:

1. What skill or ability have you developed through diligent practice? What did you learn about yourself to apply to other skill development areas?

_____

_____

_____

_____

_____

_____

_____

2. Which of your goals and peak experiences are going to need some expert coaching in order for you to accomplish them?

_____

_____

_____

_____

_____

_____

3. Which one of your goals need more dedicated practice?

_____

_____

_____

_____

4. How will you accomplish practice that is more dedicated?

_____

_____

_____

5. When will you start your ideas on the previous 4 questions?

_____

_____

_____

_____

_____

_____

Chapter 12

The Keystone Habits and Characteristics of the Happiest and Most Purposeful People and Organizations

"Don't focus on being productive; there are many unhappy but very productive people.

Focus on being purposeful. That is where true happiness, fulfillment, and effectiveness live."

~Rick Heyland

E veryone wants to be happy. But many people aren't. Depression and mental health statistics are at alarming levels.

• Approximately 1 in 5 adults in the U.S. (46.6 million) experiences mental illness in a given year.
• Approximately 1 in 25 adults in the U.S. (11.2 million) experiences a serious mental illness in a given year that substantially interferes with or limits one or more major life activities.
• Approximately 1 in 5 youth aged 13–18 (21.4%) experiences a severe mental disorder at some point during their life. For children aged 8–15, the estimate is 13%.

These types of mental health statistics are worsening in most countries around the world.

Many successful and rich people aren't happy. They have money and titles, but happiness evades them.

Why?

Is happiness a product of success? I argue no. Happiness and positivity are more likely to breed productivity and success than the other way around. In his book, *The Happiness Advantage*, Shawn Achor shares:

"We become more successful when we are happier and more positive. For example, doctors who put on a positive mood before making a diagnosis show almost three times more intelligence and creativity than doctors in a neutral state, and they make accurate diagnoses 19 percent faster. Optimistic salespeople outsell their pessimistic counterparts 56%. Students primed to feel happy before taking math achievement tests far outperform their neutral peers. It turns out that our brains are literally hardwired to perform at their best not when they are negative or even neutral, but when they are positive."

Insights like the above help us remember that happiness is the first goal.

But despite people's desire to be happy, there is so much that can get in the way of this simple pursuit. One of the most common obstacles to happiness I see is over-productivity—being overly busy or just busy on the wrong activities. Or even trickier, being busy on good things but not the best things.

I've met many people who focus on being productive to the point that they burn bridges and lose happiness. They go to sleep exhausted, not any closer to true happiness than they were when they woke up.

This raises the question: Does productivity have to come at the expense of happiness?

No, but focus on being purposeful and happiness and productivity will follow.

A few months ago, I started a survey to find out who are the most purposeful and happy people, and what habits they've adopted in their lives. I am after the holy grail of being productive, successful, and happy. We have 1,400 respondents so far. Please fill out the survey here:

https://www.surveymonkey.com/r/5ZL5MCQ

The goal is to decode the habits of those people who rank themselves at the very highest levels of happiness and the highest levels of purposefulness. There are several questions about habits, such as reading, exercise, meditation, eating, financial savings, scripture study, sleeping, etc.

Let me summarize the top characteristics and habits of the people who were the very happiest over those who were below average on happiness.

- 78% of the above average happiness group said they have a life purpose compared to 43% in the below average happiness group.
- 85% said they were content with their life as compared to 7% in the below happiness group.

- 81% said they forgive "usually or always" as compared to 37% for those in the below average group.

Their "keystone habits" of the "most happiest" as compared with the "below average" happiness group were:

- 27% higher regular exercise
- 25% more written goals
- 22% more regular service
- 27% higher in daily planning

We have already detailed the benefits and process for written goals and daily planning. Let's take a deeper look at the remaining two keystone habits–service and exercise.

Service Makes a Difference

Intuitively, we all know the value of focusing on and helping others. It is the ultimate win-win. As you think of and are kind to others, it helps you forget your problems. It feels good to connect, to help, and the other individual receives a win through your giving. We may all not be able to be a Mother Theresa, but there are benefits and "smaller steps" we can take to feel the benefits of service in our lives.

Research has long determined that conscious acts of kindness help drive increased levels of happiness. Sonja Lyubomirsky, a leading researcher and author of *The How of Happiness*, has found that individuals told to complete five acts of kindness during the course of the day report feeling much happier than control groups, and that the feeling lasts for many subsequent days, far after the act of kindness is over.

The Top 10 Ideas for Random Acts of Kindness

1. Talk with and connect with others, even if you are busy.
2. Give generous and specific compliments to others.
3. Open doors and greet strangers.
4. Call/text or visit those who are sick or afflicted.
5. Go to somebody's loved ones' funeral. Research says this is one of the most appreciated acts of kindness.
6. Do chores around the house that you're not expected to do.
7. Send a note/text to others expressing gratitude.
8. Back massage (touch).
9. Make a meal for a single friend.
10. Give small gifts to say you are thinking of them.

It just takes a little planning and a little intentionality and the love and happiness start flowing.

Lessons Learned

For Service

Planned Spontaneous Service. For some people, service is so natural. For others, we need to focus on it and be intentional. If you have a desire to be more service-oriented, try planning for it. Try including potential service activities in your daily plan. You can plan to serve those in your key relationships. You can also plan to be spontaneous with your service. For example, go into work with a plan to serve somebody. Look for opportunities to serve somebody at work. If you set the intention in your daily planning session, your brain will look for opportunities throughout the day. You can do the same thing when you get home; plan to serve somebody spontaneously.

Exercise as a Keystone Habit

I've talked about the value of exercise throughout this book. I have now correlated it with both happiness and later in this chapter with purposefulness.

The latest research on anti-aging recommends 150 to 300 minutes of moderate intensity aerobic physical activity per week, as well as at least two sessions of muscle-strengthening activity.

A team from Brigham Young University found that adults who jogged for 30 to 40 minutes five times a week had telomeres (sections of DNA) as long as those of people who were nine years younger than them, for example.

High levels of exercise appears to slow down the aging process of cells, according to this research from BYU exercise science professor, Larry Tucker.

"A person who is 45 years of age may only be 35 years of age biologically if they have a healthy lifestyle," Tucker said.

You don't have to be an athlete or compete in races to exercise. Fifty percent of the above average happiest people in my survey mentioned walking as their main exercise. Walking has tremendous cardio benefits without the wear and tear on knees, hips, and ankles.

In his book, *The Power of Habit*, author Charles Duhigg introduces a powerful concept of the keystone habit. Keystone habits are those habits that can drive success in many areas of life. He believes (as do I) that exercise is one of those keystone habits.

He says:

"Typically, people who exercise start eating better and become more productive at work. They smoke less and show more patience with colleagues and family. They use their credit cards less frequently and say they feel less stressed. Exercise is a keystone habit that triggers widespread change."

Are you ready to start or increase your exercise habit?

Duhigg also talks about other keystone habits:

"Studies have documented that families who habitually eat together seem to raise children with better homework skills, higher grades, greater emotional control, and more confidence. Making your bed every morning is correlated

with better productivity, a greater sense of well-being, and stronger skills at sticking with a budget. It's not that a family meal or a tidy bed causes better grades or less frivolous spending. But somehow, those initial shifts start chain reactions that help other good habits take hold."

My wife, Cheryl, has been practicing and preaching the making bed routine her whole life. She read a small book that reinforced her lifelong habit called, *Make Your Bed: Little Things That Can Change Your Life and Maybe Change Your World* by Admiral William H. McRaven (Ret.). He also claims that "making your bed is a keystone habit that helps kick start many other good results."

Organization Keystone Habits

After 31 years of consulting, I have learned that there are also organizational keystone habits.

They include:

1. Safety

2. Planning

Safety and Planning kick off a plethora of other habits and results.

I will share with you a story in more detail about Anil Mathur, the ex-CEO for Alaska Tanker, in the Purpose at Work chapter at the end of the book. Anil actualized a significant emotional event on one of his ships that created a new safety culture throughout the whole organization. He sent the message that safety and caring for our people was priority one. Ship cleanliness was a byproduct of improved safety and caring. Faulty equipment got fixed faster because it helped the mantra of safety and employee caring. They went on to achieve record safety, efficiency, and environmental performance because of Anil's caring attitude about people and safety.

Planning is also a keystone habit. If you take time to properly plan your work and work your plan, safety improves, quality improves, and productivity is significantly enhanced. Often planning gets overlooks because there are so many more urgent people and productivity issues to work on.

My colleagues and I at RLG International would help large organizations perform hundreds of millions of dollars in maintenance shutdowns more efficiently. The single key differential factor between 1st quartile and 4th quartile results and performance in safety, cost, and schedule was planning. If they would stay on milestone dates for quality planning despite other more urgent events going on around them, they would improve performance 25% and higher than previous shutdown events. Planning is a keystone habit for improved safety, cost, and culture. People love working for a planning culture where they are not constantly putting out fires every day.

I believe that safety, planning, regular service, and exercise are the keystone habits that effect success and productivity at work and home.

◊ ◊ ◊ ◊

As an employer, do you want people who have a life purpose? People who are happier, more forgiving, more resilient when setbacks happen who also rate significantly higher in job satisfaction?

As an individual, do you want 30% more happiness? Start living your integrated purpose statement and goals today.

I predict the "finding purpose and meaning" training business in companies will be higher in the future than 'conflict resolution' and 'good communication' combined. These results are too hard to ignore.

Develop your keystone habits for increased effectiveness.

Application Exercise:

1. Please fill out my survey at:

   https://www.surveymonkey.com/r/5ZL5MCQ

2. What did you say is your happiness level?

   _____
   _____
   _____
   _____
   _____
   _____

3. What was your service answer?

   _____
   _____
   _____
   _____

4. What was your exercise answer?

   _____
   _____
   _____
   _____

5. Which of these keystone habits are you prepared to improve upon to increase your happiness levels?

   _____
   _____
   _____

_____

_____

_____

6. 'Who' does 'What' by 'When'?

_____

_____

_____

_____

Chapter 13

Habit Synergy Through Habit Combinations

"Give me a lever long enough and a fulcrum in which to place it and I shall move the world."

~Archimedes

D o you want to move your world? Habit combinations are your lever to help move your world. The principles of leverage, working smart, and synergy are at play when you build habit combinations. We have already covered working smart in the Goals chapter. You now know about the work and dedicated practice it takes to accomplish your purpose and plans. The difficulty is, we all have limited time and energy to dedicate to practicing the skills necessary to accomplish our purpose. The principle of Habit combinations will ensure that we are maximizing our time and energy to the most effective and most efficient we can be.

The definition of synergy is the interaction or cooperation of two or more organizations, substances or other agents to produce a combined effect greater than the sum of their separate effects.

Dr. Covey talks about synergy this way: 1+1=3.

Habit combinations give you leverage and synergy while working smart. The benefit is greater than the individual parts. The morning habit routines I talked about in the daily planning chapter are habit combinations that build synergy. Start your day with the same seven to 10 activities and the benefit is much greater than the individual parts.

Imagine starting each day with an established routine that you don't even think about. It takes no brain power or willpower. It's just your routine.

James Clear in his book, *Atomic Habits: Tiny Changes, Remarkable Results* (another high recommendation), teaches about the principles of habit stacking. The principle talks about stacking an already accepted or practiced habit with a new one to help get new habits started. For example, after you brush your teeth in the morning (an already established habit), you do 10 push-ups (new habit that you want to form). Build your new habit behind an already established routine so you can get some habit synergy.

What if you could build habit combinations in the morning that could benefit you emotionally, spiritually, physically, and mentally for the rest of the day? What kind of synergy would that establish? Stephen M. R. Covey (Dr. Stephen R. Covey's son) talks about how to establish trust by keeping small commitments to yourself. In his book called, *The Speed of Trust* (another book recommendation), he writes that keeping small commitments such as getting up when the alarm clock goes off, not overeating or speaking respectfully about others -

we increase our self confidence. We build our reserves. We enlarge our capacity to make and keep greater commitments, both to ourselves and to others.

What if you could build some habit combinations into a routine that you could save time, build self-trust, increase motivation, amp up your confidence, and it takes very little cognitive load?

One of the reasons podcasts have become so popular is that you can combine them with other activities for synergistic benefit. Most podcasts are heard while working out or driving in the car or doing household chores. This is habit combinations and synergy at work.

Examples of Habit Combinations that Build Synergy

Top 10 - Morning Routine

1. Brush teeth
2. Make the bed
3. Morning prayer and/or meditation
4. Personal renewal reading (scripture or inspirational)
5. Gratitude list
6. A gratitude note to someone else (random act of kindness - service to others)
7. Daily planning (written or in phone)
8. Exercise (maybe with others to build relationships)

9. Shower
10. Breakfast

You are applying the principle of habit stacking by adding new habits in between brushing teeth and breakfast! Some benefits of these habit combinations are:

1. The physical endorphins from exercise.

2. Self confidence and self trust builds by keeping small commitments to yourself.

3. Mental and spiritual clarity from slowing down and reading, pondering, and meditating. Getting still so you can check in with your soul and your spirit.

4. Improved energy management. Save a lot of valuable cognitive energy by completing all these routines within the first hour of your day. This way, you have plenty of willpower to tackle all the hard challenges and projects coming up in the day.

5. Improved time management. While you're exercising, you can be listening to a book or doing your daily gratitude. Also, when you plan these activities separately throughout the day, it takes more time and energy and you become subject to many interruptions.

Other examples of habit combinations that create Habit synergy:

1. Our oldest daughter has a busy photography career, four kids, and her husband has a successful

career as a trial lawyer. They get Habit synergy by taking the younger two kids in the stroller for a long walk every night after dinner around her neighborhood while reviewing and planning their schedule. Exercise, nature, connection, and planning!

2. Our middle daughter just had a new baby boy. Her husband works hard and has long days from noon to 10 p.m. doing sales. They have three boys now and life is busy. She goes on a "gratitude walk" every morning with her new baby while her husband watches the older boys for an hour. She does her gratitude, listens to books, plans her day, and gets her exercise all in combination to start her day.

The real Habit synergy comes for my daughters after they have successfully completed their habit combinations. After their walks, they are more effective in their next interactions with family and work-related tasks.

Habit combination benefits are much greater than individual activities alone. The math gets exponential! This is working smart on steroids. Combine the most important activities together so you can leverage physical, emotional, spiritual, and mental health benefits all at once.

Habit combinations are not about multitasking. There are activities that you shouldn't combine. For example, don't combine listening to a podcast while writing your research paper. That will decrease synergy and productivity.

Habit combinations build synergy so your efforts are in "flow" and you can give your best effort with maximum results. To illustrate, when you study inspiring literature after meditating, it improves your clarity, awareness, and learning during your study. When you follow that with cardio exercise, it arouses your mental faculties and concentration powers.

The three hours after your mental and physical habit combinations are your most effective parts of the day! You will have concentration superpowers. This is the perfect time to do your most important or most difficult task of the day. For example, if you are a sales representative, do your cold calling for leads right after your morning habit combinations. You will experience an increased level of confidence, courage, and clarity.

That is Habit Combination Synergy!

Application Exercise:

1. What habit combinations would provide synergy in your life?

_____

_____

_____

_____

Chapter 14

Why do so few people have and live an articulated purpose?

I am fascinated to study and research why more people don't work to develop and articulate their purpose.

In a 2014 Harvard Business Review article by Nick Craig and Scott A. Snook entitled, "From Purpose to Impact", it cited that fewer than 20% of leaders have a strong sense of their own individual purpose. "Even fewer can distill their purpose into a concrete statement," the authors state. "They may be able to clearly articulate their organization's mission: Think of Google's "To organize the world's information and make it universally accessible and useful", or Charles Schwab's "A relentless ally for the individual investor". But when asked to describe their own purpose, they typically fall back on something generic and nebulous: "Help others excel." "Ensure success." "Empower my people." Just as problematic, hardly any of them have a clear plan for translating purpose into action. As a result, they limit their aspirations and often fail to achieve their most ambitious professional and personal goals."

Later in the article they go on to say, "Indeed, we believe that the process of articulating your purpose and finding the courage to live it - what we call purpose to impact - is the single most important developmental task you can undertake as a leader. Many who do articulate their purpose have seen dramatic results, ranging from two-step promotions to sustained improvement in business results. Most importantly, the vast majority tell us they've developed a new ability to thrive in even the most challenging times."

I completely agree. Do you want to show up strong at your job? Do you want do rise to the top? Do you want to be a better parent or partner? Do you want to live a more fulfilling life? Then develop your purpose and live it. This section attempts to review some of the potential concerns or roadblocks that people have on developing and living their purpose, and my ideas on solutions.

I believe the biggest reasons that people are not living their purpose are twofold:

1. They don't know how to articulate it and live it. The uncertainty of how to develop or discover their purpose creates anxiety. This book so far has been an attempt to give you a step-by-step process to find it, articulate it, and to put it into action every day.
2. People get discouraged because of setbacks and don't have a strategy to overcome discouragement, fatigue, anxiety, and setbacks to accomplish their purpose and goals.

According to a study out of the University of Pennsylvania, as we pursue our purpose, it induces more anxiety. "The Search for Purpose in Life: An Exploration of Purpose, the Search Process, and Purpose Anxiety" by Larissa Yvonne Rainey says:

"Results indicated that the vast majority of people crave a sense of purpose in life, but nearly always encounter purpose anxiety during their search process, no matter the searcher's age. Results also showed that purpose anxiety significantly hampers wellbeing. This project (research paper) in no way intends to suggest that individuals should avoid searching for purpose. Rather, it merely means to enhance psychology's knowledge of the search process so that interventions may be developed to prevent or mitigate the psychological distress that so often accompanies the struggle for purpose in life."

This section is written to give the right mindset, toolset, and skillset to stay on plan and on purpose. Its aim is to help you overcome stress, anxiety, and accomplish great things in your life.

Application Exercise:

1. Have you ever stopped setting goals in the past?

   _____

   _____

   _____

2. If yes, then why?

   _____

   _____

   _____

3. Have you experienced anxiety and stress while setting or trying to accomplish your purpose or compelling goals?

   _____

   _____

   _____

   _____

4. If yes, how did you cope? What would you do differently?

   _____

   _____

   _____

   _____

   _____

   _____

Chapter 15

An Approach to Overcome Setbacks and Stress and to Stay on Purpose

So you have your purpose statement, you have set your yearly goals, you are perfecting your weekly and daily planning systems, and you get fired from your job unexpectedly. Alternatively, you have not been able to save as much money for your house as you had planned. Or, you're experiencing a setback in any one of your chosen goals. Perhaps you're even experiencing some level of anxiety developing your purpose statement and goals. What do you do? Give up? Say that goal setting doesn't work? That defining your purpose isn't worth it? Get mad at yourself? Get depressed?

From Larissa Rainey: "Researchers found small to medium correlations between the searches for meaning and negative affect, depression, and neuroticism when surveying undergraduate college students. They found that while the *presence* of meaning is positively associated with life satisfaction, happiness, and positive affect and negatively associated with depression and negative affect, the *search* for meaning is negatively correlated with life satisfaction, happiness, and positive affect and positively correlated with depression and negative affect."

These same researchers furthered this line of research, discovering that individuals who reported high levels of the search for meaning were protected from the negative outcomes of the search process if they had high levels of self-actualization. Together, these studies indicate that having a strong sense of meaning in life and fulfilling the need for self-actualization may negate the detrimental effects of the search process. Also, these researchers hadn't gone through the same "Triple 7" development process that you now have!

The process is worth the effort! With any powerful and effective medicine, there are side effects. Do the benefits outweigh the side effects? In this case, clearly yes! We just need to be aware of the potential side effects or setbacks and make a plan to overcome them.

The need for the right mindset, skillset, and toolset to overcome anxiety and setbacks.

I worked for three years counseling young adults (ages 18 to 30) who had addiction problems of various kinds. They would often recount to me that the "suck it up and try harder" method does not work. When they received counsel that said try harder, get more grit, be tougher minded, it never worked. What these young people with addiction problems needed was a new mindset, skillset, and toolset to overcome their problems. You may not have an addiction to beat, but we all need a clear approach to stay on purpose and overcome discouragement and anxiety.

My personal experience with coping with stress and anxiety.

In approximately 2005 when I was in my mid-forties, I had a realization that there was something missing from my "live your purpose" model. I was at the pinnacle of my career; promotions happened and with each promotion came the need for more travel. I was traveling over 100 nights per year for many years. I went back to my purpose statement and knew I was still living my purpose and accomplishing my goals, but something was missing. I couldn't exercise more to help cope; I was running marathons at the time. I knew I could not fit more into my life. I had already found God but was sometimes having trouble hearing him and feeling him.

I had a few symptoms that told me I wasn't handling all the stress of my "successful" lifestyle. I was "short" with my wife and kids during high stress periods. I also started to watch more TV than I usually did at night. While traveling, I started every day at 5 a.m. with my morning routines and then finished by 7 p.m. or 8 p.m. after serving employees and clients all day. I was exhausted!

Somebody told me about mindfulness and meditation, but I didn't pay it any attention. However, after a stress breakdown in my hotel room one night, I went looking for help. It was then that I picked up a book by Eckhart Tolle called the *Power of Now*. I had to read the book four times to let it sink in. It was like a different language to me, foreign from the western ideals and teachings I had been trained in.

My dad, Dale, also found value in this book. We put together our top lessons from it together.

Here are the top 10 lessons to learn from *The Power of Now* on becoming more mindful:

1. Say yes to life, accept challenges, and watch how life starts working for you.

2. Whatever the present moment contains, accept it as if we had chosen it. Make the present our friend - not our enemy. This will transform our lives.

3. Being free (being separate from the dictates of our mind) is an important skill. Freedom and peace come with the realization that our thoughts are a separate process within us.

4. We as individuals are not the thought generators. Our mind is a resource to us, and we can observe our thoughts. When we do this, a higher level of consciousness becomes activated and we make better choices.

   For example, if someone offends us, notice how the mind takes over and provides all sorts of negative support, such as, "I've never liked that person. They have the nerve to treat me like this," and the negative ideas continue to flow. Therefore, we need to be alert that not everything our mind feeds us is for our wellbeing. We need to be separate from our thoughts, stand back and observe them, rather than just accept them. We must be aware of them, and decide if they are helpful, peaceful, or if we need to let them go in order for peace and happiness to grow within us.

5. Love, joy, and peace cannot flourish until we are freed from mind dominance.

6. Resentment, hatred, self-pity, guilt, anger, depression, jealousy, etc. and even the slightest irritation are creations of the mind. In other words, the unobserved mind can run our lives.

7. We must focus our attention on the feelings inside us. Stay present and continue to be an observer of what is happening to you. The power of NOW is the power of our own conscious presence of what is occurring.

8. Once we have understood the basic principle of being present in the NOW as a watcher of what happens inside us—and understand it by experiencing it—we have at our disposal the most potent transformational tool: we can let ideas go and not own them.

9. Anyone who is only identified with their mind is therefore disconnected from their true power and deeper self-rooted person.

10. Stop living in the past (whether positive or negative) or looking for happiness in the future. NOW is the most precious time. NOW is a thing that will take us beyond the confines of our mind.

This stuff blew my mind. I was too mind dominant. I was too ego-mind-driven. I had never even heard about being an observer or staying in the present moment. Look at number 9 above. That learning really hit me hard. I was letting my mind and ego dominance disconnect me from my purpose and true power. This book and its concepts were like trying to learn a new language and a new skillset.

I have since read many Eastern philosophy authors such as Deepak Chopra and Wayne Dyer. I started to see how this could fit with my purpose, goals, and planning. It was the missing piece. Accepting "setbacks" in your life or not judging them is opposite to what we learn in life. Mindfulness and other tools are available to overcome stress, anxiety, and depression.

I'll conclude this chapter with a quote from Larissa Rainey's academic paper on the search for purpose:

"While some individuals do effortlessly happen upon and live out their purpose, many struggle to discover, understand, and fulfill their "why" for living. As the present study indicated, this search for purpose can be psychologically taxing at any stage of life—spurring significant stress, anxiety, worry, and frustration and thoroughly dampening every element of individual wellbeing for nearly all who search for purpose.

"All that being said, it seems obvious that the benefits of having a strong sense of purpose in life ultimately outweigh the negatives of purpose anxiety. The pain of struggling for purpose will be well worth it, for it is purposeful living that gives meaning to life and positively affects one's emotional landscape, engagement, relationships, and sense of achievement."

To overcome the anxiety that can come from developing purpose or just overcoming life's setbacks and the struggle to live your best life, I recommend three practices. Building a skillset in these three areas will help overcome any setbacks and get back to purpose!

1. A mindfulness practice
2. A gratitude practice
3. An acceptance practice.

With these three skills, you'll be able to stay on purpose.

Lessons Learned

Every day is New Year's Day! Don't you love people's attitude about a new year? There is always a party and celebration - a renewed feeling of hope. People set new goals. Gyms are always packed with people that have made new commitments for the future. What if we took that attitude into each new day?

Each new day is a new start. Even if you had a hard day the day before, each new day is a fresh start to try again. After a good night's sleep, start each day with hope and a sense of renewal.

Chapter 16

Build a Mindfulness Practice Through Meditation

Mindfulness is the psychological process of purposely bringing one's attention to experiences occurring in the present moment without judgment, which one develops through the practice of meditation and through other training.

Mindfulness is not a religion, but is simply a method of mental training. Mindfulness is such a great way to develop the skills and tools to deal with adversity and find sustaining happiness. In the last few years, there has been more and more research showing the demonstrable benefits of mindfulness through meditation.

Mira Rakicevic in her blog lists, 'Meditation Statistics That You Should be Aware of' and does a great job collating 27 benefits of meditation (according to Project-Meditation, The Good Body, and The National Center for Biotechnical Information). A partial listing of her meditation statistics and benefits are as follows:

1. It's estimated that 200–500 million people meditate worldwide.

In recent years, the meditation stats show that the practice has been gaining in popularity.

Considering all the health benefits it offers, it's no surprise that an increasing number of people use it.

(The Good Body)

2. Over 14% of Americans have meditated at least once.

Additionally, the Pew Research Center's research indicates that this percentage could actually be much higher with 40% of U.S. adults meditating at least once a week.

(The Good Body)

3. In 2017, 14.2% of U.S. adults said that they had meditated in the past 12 months.

The CDC's report, "Use of Yoga, Meditation, and Chiropractors Among U.S. Adults Aged 18 and Older" is a great source of relevant meditation statistics for 2017. According to its findings, the percentage of people who use meditation has increased considerably from 2012, when only 4.1% of Americans had meditated the previous year.

The report's authors explained this sharp rise by an increase in the number of meditation and yoga cellphone apps. Additionally, there are more and more companies and schools offering yoga and meditation classes to their employees and students.

(Centers for Disease Control and Prevention)

Benefits of Meditation

4. The majority of people practice meditation to improve their general wellness.

About 76% of people using meditation said that general wellness is their primary motive. Other reasons they meditate include boosting energy levels (60%), improving memory and focus (50%), and relieving anxiety, stress, and depression.

(The Good Body)

5. Meditation improves anxiety levels 60% of the time.

After meditating for 6–9 months, almost two-thirds of those prone to anxiety managed to reduce their anxiety levels.

(Project-Meditation)

6. Meditation can reduce the risk of being hospitalized for coronary disease by 87%.

Meditation studies reveal that people who meditate are less likely to suffer from heart disease. Since meditation is a kind of relaxation technique, it relieves stress, which is a well-known cause of many serious medical conditions.

(Project-Meditation)

7. Meditation relieves the symptoms of insomnia 75% of the time.

The majority of people with insomnia who meditated on a daily basis were able to fall asleep more quickly. In fact, 75% of them needed only up to 20 minutes to doze off. Additionally, 91% of insomniacs reduced or completely eliminated their use of sleeping medication.

(Project-Meditation)

There is some research by Project Meditation that shows that meditation can increase employees' productivity by 120%. Additionally, employers who introduced meditation to their employees claim that work absenteeism decreased by 85% while profits increased by 520%.

Are you convinced? Are you ready to start your own mediation practice? If not, here is more empirical evidence:

Danny Penman and Mark Williams wrote a great book called, *Mindfulness: An Eight-Week Plan for Finding Peace in a Frantic World.*

Williams and Penman said, "Numerous psychological studies have shown that regular meditators are happier and more contented than average. These are not just important results in themselves, but have huge medical significance, as such positive emotions are linked to a longer and healthier life."

They go on to say that anxiety, depression, and irritability all decrease with regular sessions of meditation. Memory also improves, reaction times become faster, and mental and physical stamina increase. Regular meditators enjoy better and more fulfilling relationships. I could go on with other countless studies and benefits, but you get the point. Meditation is a wonder drug!

Meditation is a terrific skill and tool to help you to stay present and mindful without judgment. However, like anything else, it needs practice. I love the way in yoga and meditation that they use the word, practice. Any good skill needs practice.

It takes deliberate practice to become good at staying mindful. Recently, I did a review of three popular meditation apps. I reviewed Calm, Mindfulness, and 10% Happier. My findings are below where I compared the features, pricing, pros, and cons.

Here is the quick side-by-side comparison.

App Name	10% Happier	Calm	The Mindfulness App
Free Trial Pricing	7 Days $99/year	7 Days $70/year	7 Days $59/year
Key Contributors	Dan Harris and other top meditation experts	Tamara Levitt	Martin Wikfalk
Special Contributors	Daily Covid-19 3 p.m. meditations	Lebron James discussing an Intro to Mental Fitness	A plethora of contributors

App Name	10% Happier	Calm	The Mindfulness App
Special Features	Weekly Podcast	Rate your mood feature and daily gratitude list	Library filled with premium meditations and courses
Favorite Feature	Breadth of topics and teachers	Daily calm meditation to do in the morning on different topics	Wide variety of topics and teachers
Least Favorite Feature	Higher cost and Dan's podcasts can be too long to listen to	None	The app isn't as well organized and its rating system isn't as useful as Calm
Overall Value Rank	8/10	10/10	6/10

Comparing these meditation apps was very enjoyable for me. I had to listen and learn from the best mindfulness teachers and practitioners.

I came into this analysis as a long-time 10% Happier supporter. However, my recent decision is that Calm is currently the best meditation app. Tamara Levitt's early morning 10-minute Daily Calm messages are fantastic, and I learned something new every day. Today's topic could be on change, and yesterday's on acceptance. Tamera's voice is so soothing, making it a relaxed early morning listen.

I especially like Calm's rating systems. You can rate your mood at any time throughout your day, and then Calm recommends which meditation to listen to. This simple, AI-based feature is a game-changer. I also love using the daily gratitude reminder in the morning and at night. The icing on the cake was listening to Lebron James and his mental fitness messages.

Meditation is an important part of a healthy high-performance lifestyle. This is a fundamental behavior for staying on purpose.

Today, the mindfulness and meditation business is a billion dollar plus industry, but only 14% of people in the U.S. have tried meditation, according to a 2017 CDC report. This is up from 4.1% in 2012. Although it is growing fast, it clearly is not catching on with the majority.

If you can't commit to a regular meditation practice, try 2-minute breathing time-outs.

Try deep breathing 10 times. Nice long 'in breaths' and nice long 'out breaths'. Try it now ...

Do you feel more relaxed? Does it calm you in that moment? Deep breathing is a such a valuable tool in a busy day. Try taking breathing timeouts in the car or walking down the hallway or when you get a drink. High performance coach Brendon Burchard and author of *High Performance Habits* says that high performers have a habit of "release tension, set intention".

His process is as follows:

1. Close your eyes.
2. Repeat the word 'release' in your mind over and over. Breathe deeply and release the tension over your whole body.
3. When you feel you've released some tension, set intention. This means think about what you want to feel and achieve in the next activity.

Think about doing this type of breathing time-out during 2-minute intervals at transitions in your day:

- From home to work
- From work to home
- From one meeting to the next
- For a big presentation
- When talking with your spouse or kids
- Before talking to your boss
- When you go out on a date

Relax, take deep breaths, and ask, how do I want to show up during this next part of my day? Do I want to show up with love and compassion? Do I want to listen for understanding?

This skill of mindfulness fits in so nicely with living purposefully. Be purposeful and intentional in everything you do! Show up "on purpose" through improved mindfulness.

Lessons Learned

"3 a Day" during Covid-19

I am still a novice in the mindfulness practice. When Covid-19 started in 2020, I set a goal to increase my mediation practice. I wanted to go from doing one 10-minute mediation daily to 3-10 minute meditations per day. My primary goals during this experiment were to increase my calmness under stress and to improve my sleep. This was a difficult time to test the benefits of increased meditation during the unsettling times that the virus presented and while writing this book. Nevertheless, I did improve my sleep (an increase of 28 minutes per night) and significantly improved the "calm under pressure".

The calmness may not stay, but then with 10 minutes of mindful breathing, you can find peace again.

Application Exercise:

1. Are you ready to start a meditation practice?

    _____
    _____
    _____
    _____

2. Which app will you use?

    _____
    _____
    _____

3. Are you ready to start "2-minute breathing timeouts"?

    _____
    _____
    _____
    _____
    _____

4. If so, 'What' and 'When'?

    _____
    _____
    _____
    _____

Chapter 17

Build a Gratitude Practice to Stay Purposeful

"Gratitude is not only the greatest of virtues, but the parent of all the others."

~Marcus Tullius Cicero

A skilled gratitude practice is another skill to help you stay on purpose. Gratitude is defined as the quality of being thankful; a readiness to show appreciation for and to return kindness.

The self-critic inside is so powerful, we need a skill to overcome the critic and stay focused on progress, not just achievement. A good gratitude practice helps accomplish that.

Every day for the last several years, I start my morning with a gratitude list of three to six things that I'm grateful for. It really helps me focus on my blessings and the things I have versus those I don't have.

Gratitude is the ultimate win-win strategy as it benefits the individual at home and at work.

In an article by Dr. Charles D. Kerns titled, "Gratitude at Work: Counting your Blessings Will Benefit You and Your Organization", it says,

"Gratitude is not just a "feel good" emotion when it comes to organizational life. It can benefit an organization in many ways. When an employee believes his or her superiors are grateful for his or her work, the employee will benefit by having an improved sense of worth to the organization. This improved sense of worth can lead to performance improvement, thereby benefiting the organization.

"For instance, research has shown that persons who are genuinely grateful may be more optimistic, experience improved health, and perhaps even have extended life spans. All of these benefits also potentially benefit the organization for which that person works."

Dr. Kerns continues, "Growing evidence indicates that the expression of gratitude can also improve one's physical health and researchers are finding that behaviors such as gratitude, for example, may be reliably connected to positive changes in an individual's cardiovascular and immune functioning. In one recent study, individuals who focused on being grateful rather than on not being angry were found to positively affect a variety of important physiological functions such as improved heart pulse, and respiration rates. It would seem that the practice of gratitude might hold promise for reducing stress and consequent related health care costs, which in an organizational setting could bring great dividends."

There is a terrific research study called the "31 Benefits of Gratitude: The Ultimate Science-Backed Guide." I encourage you to read it online at: https://www.happierhuman.com/benefits-of-gratitude/

The 31 benefits include emotional, social, personality, health, and career. The study shows a 10% improvement in happiness through daily gratitude writing.

Gratitude at Work

Adrian Gostick and Chester Elton wrote a terrific book called, *Leading with Gratitude: Eight Leadership Practices for Extraordinary Business Results* (another book I highly recommend).

Their research shows a gratitude gap at work. Despite the overwhelming evidence of the benefits of gratitude, the skill is not fully utilized at work. Adrian and Chester's book shares examples of how increased gratitude at work can improve morale, productivity, job satisfaction, and profitability. One of the examples shared in the book pertained to the WD-40 Company. When leadership gave thousands of managers training in expressing gratitude to their employees, the company saw record increases in revenue. I highly recommend their book for anyone trying to improve gratitude at work or home.

To help enhance your own personal, family, and/or organizational gratitude practice, here are some ideas:

Start each day with gratitude. Write down in your journal or day planner what and whom you are grateful for. The writing (or typing) activity helps the brain more clearly register what you are grateful for.

Start each meeting with positive recognition. Give people a chance to recognize positive behavior of others before your next weekly or monthly meeting. It may take a time or two before people come prepared, but after two or three tries, it will transform the feeling of the meeting and the people involved.

Write gratitude notes to family or employees. Write a note or a letter expressing gratitude. In our Corporate Anniversary Letters at RLG to our employees, we always included a gratitude note to highlight what we are grateful for with that employee. We have received very positive feedback from our employees and their spouses.

Endorse and recognize others on social media platforms such as LinkedIn, Facebook or Instagram. People love to see their name in lights on social media. LinkedIn endorsements are a great way to broadcast people's strengths and contributions outside of the company.

Write customer appreciation letters. This was the original intent of chocolates at Christmas to your customers. Don't let a gift to a customer or a key supplier go out without a personalized gratitude note.

Monthly or weekly reports that start with recognition of others. Have a section on every monthly report from your staff that highlights the positive efforts or results of others. I promise every report will be read and reviewed.

Recognition by walking around. Go catch people doing things right. Take time each day or week to go and catch people doing things right in their work environment. Nothing can motivate a young employee more than their boss coming to their work area and thanking them for their efforts and results.

Solicit ungrateful feedback. Ask your employees or family members for feedback. When have I been ungrateful? Ungrateful actions are hard to recognize without coaching from others.

The research cited above indicates that people with gratitude can create superior work outcomes, have stronger social supports, have more energy and better health, stronger immune systems, lower stress levels, and live longer.

Application Exercise:

1. What are you grateful for?

   _____
   _____
   _____
   _____
   _____
   _____

2. How is your gratitude practice? Rate it from 1-5 (5 being excellent).

   _____
   _____

3. What one thing will you start doing to improve your gratitude practice?

   _____
   _____
   _____
   _____
   _____
   _____

4. Gratitude Action Plan: 'Who' does 'What' by 'When'?

   _____
   _____
   _____
   _____

Chapter 18

Build an Acceptance Practice to Stay Purposeful

The last piece of the purposeful model for sustained happiness and fulfillment is the practice of Acceptance. This idea will be a bit foreign to some. Acceptance is really mindfulness, gratitude, and meditation put into practice. We are usually taught when setbacks happen, we fight harder, we buckle down, and never give up. Or, we give up, get depressed and discouraged, and give up on our goals and dreams. The practice of acceptance does not mean we just accept everything that happens to us. It also doesn't mean we stay in very bad situations. It means we are mindful, observant, and accept what has happened so we can best respond.

Here is Noah Rasheta, a lay Buddhist teacher's explanation of acceptance. He compares acceptance to a game of Tetris.

"I want to be completely clear about the concept of acceptance and again clarify that the Buddhist understanding of acceptance does not encourage or condone in any way resignation or disengagement. If you are in an abusive relationship, acceptance is NOT in any way an attitude of saying, "Oh well, I'm not going to do anything about this." Alternatively, "It is what it is." Acceptance is simply recognizing, "Ok, this is the situation I'm in. Now what am I going to do with it?" It is seeing the new Tetris piece and immediately recognizing, "Ok, this is the shape I have, now what do I do with it?" If you do not want to go through life in a state of constant reactivity (you know, yelling at the game "I don't want this shape"), then you need to learn to accept what is and then you have the freedom to respond. Therefore, acceptance is the key to having the freedom to respond."

Russ Harris, who wrote *The Happiness Trap: How to Stop Struggling and Start Living: A Guide to ACT* (another high reading recommendation), has great examples on how to use the ACT model to put mindfulness and acceptance to work in your life.

The ACT model is:

A= Accept your thoughts and feelings and be present
C= Connect with your purpose and values (on how you want to respond)
T= Take effective action

Doesn't that make sense? A setback happens, we observe it and we accept it so we can properly respond rather than get stuck. We then connect to our purpose and best self, decide how we want to respond, and take action.

Let's use a real-life problem using the ACT model. Let's say you are discouraged about how your boss is treating you at work. He is always giving you negative feedback about your work. Then when you deliver sales above quota, he hardly notices. You believe potential promotions have been negatively affected as a result. You could get angry, resentful, and become overly obsessed with what he is saying or thinking. This will only lead to mental duress and pain.

If you follow the ACT model:

Accept your thoughts and feelings and be present. Accept that you have been given difficult feedback. Accept that positive recognition has not come your way when quotas have been achieved and exceeded. It is what it is. The only way to not become too mind-obsessed is to accept what *is*. Be a neutral observer of what is happening. Try not to put judgments and labels on what is happening. Now you have the freedom to respond.

Connect with your purpose and values. How do you really want to respond? How would your best self respond? Read over your purpose statement. How should you respond based on your purpose? Remember Robert Mason's purpose statement from chapter four?

Here it is:

"To live a bold, empowered life full of God's grace and favor that allows me to see yet to be imagined victories and cultivate that future today, through perseverance, integrity, respect, and collaboration. A future full of possibilities for myself, my family, and those around me."

If Robert is going to respond to his boss based on his purpose statement, how should he respond?

He should respond with perseverance, integrity, respect, and collaboration. (Btw, I know Robert and that is exactly how he would respond)

In this example, Robert can't control his boss. Robert can only control how he responds. After looking at his purpose, he knows he should respond with respect, integrity, perseverance, and collaboration. Do you see the power of defining your purpose? It isn't just something that helps you find a job. It's a guidepost to help you cope and deal with life's most difficult challenges.

Take effective action: What action should Robert take to stay present? What action is consistent with his purpose and best self? He might talk to his boss and share his honest and vulnerable feelings and then let it go. How can Robert show his boss respect? Bosses aren't perfect and we shouldn't hold them to a standard that is unattainable. What stress is his boss under? What can Robert do to help his boss? How can Robert collaborate in a different way with him? Ask the boss. These types of questions will lead you to peace and value-based responses and actions.

Let's look at another home and family example using the ACT model. Let's imagine you are struggling with your father (or in any strained family relationship that you might be struggling with). In your eyes, your father has been less than accepting of you and your family. He has judged you and it has hurt your feelings. It's getting to the point that you don't want to be around him because he might say something hurtful.

Accept your thoughts and feelings and be present.

Accept what happened. Acknowledge your feelings. They are how you feel. Don't fight how you feel. Observe how you feel. Don't put labels on it. They are just words. Allow the thoughts and feelings to come and go, but don't lock them down. Let them pass. Accept, stay present. Now you are free to respond with your values.

Connect with your values. How do you really want to respond? How would you respond based on your purpose and best self? As Eckhart Tolle would say, "Let go of your ego. Don't let your ego respond. Let your purpose and values respond."

Remember Nola's purpose statement from chapter four? Here it is again:

"I am a creator. I create beauty and happiness in my world. I am a connector. I make meaningful connections in my relationships and my physical world. I am strong. I gain strength and wisdom from my mistakes and past experiences."

How would Nola respond based on her purpose? (Btw, she has a great relationship with her father). She wants meaningful connections in her relationships. She desires happiness and to learn from her mistakes. How can she connect with her father? She would desire an open conversation with her father to express her real feelings. Before she has the conversation, she could remind herself what she has learned from her father. How has he contributed to her beauty and happiness? This frame of mind will help make the conversation more productive. Meditating on these questions will allow her to connect to her purpose and respond appropriately.

Take appropriate action: Have the courage to take action according to your values. Go in and share with your father all the things you are grateful for. Then share what is hurting. If you share it with gratitude and compassion in your heart, he will understand. Share with your father the lines from your purpose statement. Tell him you want a great connection and a great relationship. Seek to understand what you can do differently. I am willing to bet this could change the nature of the conversation. And worst case, if he doesn't, you have done the right thing and were consistent with your values. You will build confidence and courage as you respond based on your values even if it doesn't initially work out the way you planned.

◊ ◊ ◊ ◊

Dr. Harris provides an excellent summary of ACT and of the journey I have been trying to take you through. "There is an ancient Eastern saying: "If you don't decide where you're going, you'll end up wherever you're heading." To live a meaningful life, you need direction, and your values are there deep in your heart to provide it." So, connect with those values – use them for guidance. Cultivate a sense of purpose. Keep setting meaningful goals and pursue them vigorously. At the same time, appreciate what you have in your life right now. And remember, life gives most to those who make the most of what life gives.

Please don't be discouraged if you don't accomplish your goals on the first attempt. The mindfulness and acceptance practice has taught us to focus on setting goals, but not to focus on the outcomes. Be grateful for what you have accomplished and accept what setbacks happen. Continue to learn and practice. The joy is in the journey. The joy is in the process. If you will enjoy the journey and keep learning, you'll eventually accomplish all of your goals. Some of these skills take practice. Be curious and open to develop great practice habits.

Lessons Learned

Seek to understand before being understood. Dr. Covey taught this idea well in his "7 Habits" book. I remember being so upset at an undergraduate professor. I had received a grade I thought I definitely didn't deserve. I had worked very hard on this particular test.

It was a Tuesday and Thursday organizational behavior class. He handed out the grade at the end of Thursday's class. I was smoking mad. Honestly, I didn't respect this professor very much and this put me over the top. I was going to go give him a piece of my mind, but there was a line-up of students to see him after this Thursday class and I had an appointment across town. This happened before I had my purpose statement and before I knew about ACT.

But I did have a loving and caring wife. After I went home, Cheryl did her best to calm me down and help me see things from his point of view and with a bit more perspective. I pondered a lot over the weekend on how I might respond to this professor. I softened my approach based on time to "cool off" - Cheryl's advice and an instinct to seek his opinion first. I had read Dr. Covey's advice of, "Seek first to understand before being understood". I went into class early the next Tuesday and sought to understand from the professor what he was looking for on each section of the test. I did let him know how hard I had worked. We spent 30 minutes together with him doing most of the talking. As he was talking, he was re-looking at my responses. I could see that he was liking what he was reading. By the end of the discussion, he bumped my test to an "A". He apologized for missing critical information and mentioned how busy he was and what a big course and consulting load he had that semester.

I have since learned that in any relationship conflict, to seek first to understand with real empathy for the other person's position always works better than giving them a "piece of your mind". The giving them a "piece of your mind" strategy might feel good for about 5 minutes, but then you have either lost a relationship or it may take months or years to repair that relationship.

Application Exercise:

1.What difficult situation are you dealing with
right now?

_____

_____

_____

_____

   a. How can you accept your thoughts and
feelings and stay present?

      _____

      _____

      _____

      _____

   b. How would you respond based on your
purpose and values?

      _____

      _____

      _____

      _____

      _____

      _____

   c. Take effective action. What action should
you take?

      _____

      _____

      _____

      _____

      _____

171

SECTION I   **Why Purpose**

SECTION II   **How to Develop Purpose**

SECTION III   **Plan to Live Your Purpose**

SECTION IV   **Purposeful Practice**

SECTION V   **Staying on Purpose**

SECTION VI   **Purpose at Work**

Live Your Purpose

Chapter 19

Purpose at Work

"Companies that understand the increasing emphasis of purpose in today's professional landscape improve their ability to attract such employees and also their ability to retain them for longer periods of time."

~Reid Hoffman, Executive Chairman and co-founder, LinkedIn

I couldn't write a book on purpose without specifically talking about the importance of purpose at work. The average person spends 90,000 hours at work over their lifetime which equates to 33% of our lives. We need to be more intentional about making work purposeful both as an individual and from a leadership perspective.

I have always marveled how the very best and most successful companies have a clear purpose and a clear 'why'. Most companies with average performances focus on the 'what' and 'how' they do what they do.

LinkedIn commissioned the largest global study in 2016 of the importance of purpose at work. They found that 85% of the companies who had a clear purpose showed positive growth. They also found that 42% of companies without a clear purpose saw a reduction in revenue - further evidence that purpose is just as important at work.

Many people admire Apple. We love their products. We love their designs, but that isn't the real reason they're so successful. The real reason is that they do not describe 'what' they do; in other words, we make computers, etc. They describe their core purpose and their why. Their purpose was originally to be a disruptor. It was to be the anti-IBM. IBM's advertisements were with people in suits and ties. Apple's advertisements were with people dressed much more casually. Apple wanted to challenge the status quo. They wanted to get a computer in every household. They were anti-establishment. Since that time, they have expanded their purpose to include "a disruptor in every business category they enter into". If you own an Apple product, you are part of this brand. It is their superpower. It's why people line up for hours to get their latest products.

Here is the original Mission Statement developed for Apple Computer Inc. by Steve Jobs and Steve Wozniak on January 3, 1977:

Apple is dedicated to the empowerment of man—to making personal computing accessible to each and every individual so as to help change the way we think, work, learn, and communicate.

Wow! Talk about purpose. The empowerment of man, available to everybody and changing the way we work, learn, and communicate. They have literally changed the world as we know it because of the power of purpose!

Business 'why' expert Simon Sinick says it this way: "Apple and every company that has loyalty from their customers, investors, and employees start with why! **The WHY is the purpose, cause or belief that drives every one of us.**"

If Apple can demand market dominance and superiority from a strong 'why', shouldn't our companies and we find our 'Why' or purpose?

◊ ◊ ◊ ◊

The January 2013 McKinsey Quarterly had an article by Susie Cranston and Scott Keller called, "Increasing the Meaning Quotient of Work." They argue that the most successful and best performing people or companies have IQ (intellectual quotient), EQ (emotional quotient), and MQ (meaning quotient).

The authors say, "While IQ and EQ are absolutely necessary to create the conditions for peak performance, they are far from sufficient. When a business environment MQ is low, employees put less energy into their work and see it as "just a job" that gives them little more than a paycheck."

The executives interviewed in the study said that when employees and teams that have IQ, EQ and MQ, they are five times more productive. What's more, when they asked executives to locate the bottlenecks to peak performance in organizations, more than 90% choose MQ-related issues.

Given this information, how do we develop organizational meaning and purpose?

For leaders in companies, I would argue that developing your individual purpose is critical as you influence hundreds and maybe thousands of employees. Please spend the time to develop a clear purpose as described in the Triple 7 process in chapter four. To be purposeful has such a great multiplier effect in a company. You can positively or negatively influence so many lives.

Organization purpose is more difficult to create because of the number of people involved or not involved. It is easier to find meaning if you're a tech company who is going to change the world like Apple and Google who organize the world's information. They have an easier time creating meaning and purpose that inspires discretionary effort. What if you're not a tech company? How do you inspire meaning and five times more productivity?

Ideas to Enhance Organizational Meaning and Purpose.

1. When you speak about your company, share how the product helps provide meaning to all the stakeholders: e.g. society, the customer, the team, and themselves.

   "You don't just make lumber."

My very first client as a young consultant was a sawmill supervisor named Greg. He was a great athlete and loved to compete and win. Greg and I spent a few night shifts at the plant trying to figure out how to advance performance there. Greg continued to work at the plant for over 30 years. He advanced from supervisor to superintendent to plant manager. That plant went on to be one of the top performing sawmills of its category in North America. He did at least two things that were extraordinary: He always had employee and management meetings. He rarely skipped a weekly employee meeting and his monthly management business review for 30 years. Talk about consistency!

Everybody is always trying to create some stability and sustainability for performance in their business. Try learning this lesson from Greg. Never skip a performance review and business discussion. He was also a great communicator on multiple levels of meaning. He talked to his employees about things that would draw them into the business and care about its performance. He would share the details of financial and production performance to the union employees on a weekly basis. As a result, the plant took great pride and meaning in trying to become the best sawmill. He would tie in customer feedback into his meetings. He would share the good and the bad. He built pride, meaning, and loyalty to the site. I think it was one of the reasons he never left, despite being offered other positions at other plants. My

> "Nothing else can quite substitute for a few well-chosen, well-timed, sincere words of praise. They're absolutely free - and worth a fortune."

> ~Sam Walton, founder of Walmart

favorite line he ever said was in a weekly employee meeting when he passionately shared with his employees that they "don't just make lumber". They provide shelter for those less fortunate and would talk about the Habitat for Humanity project in the local town that the company donated to. He would talk about how their product helped people live their dreams of being a homeowner. Greg did establish a culture of meaning and pride by connecting the company's product to how it benefited society, the customers, and themselves.

2. Do small but meaningful activities to create meaning and purpose beyond the paycheck.

"Flowers on your Partner's Birthday"

When I got into the consulting business over 30 years ago, I often heard from managers that we do not need positive employee recognition. Employees get their paycheck and that is enough. My response was always, "There are two types of people: those who need and like positive recognition, and liars!" Fortunately, our leadership philosophies are so much more advanced today. Today, we all recognize that what Sam Walton was saying above is true. We do sometimes still struggle with the execution of the recognition idea. It does not have to be a big deal, but it does have to be sincere and specific.

At RLG International, we had a practice of sending home flowers on an employee's partner's birthday and a specific recognition note sent to the home on the employee's company anniversary date. The note was always accompanied by a 'dinner out' coupon and some specific praise and recognition about the last year. After 30 years, the company still gets regular communication back from spouses and partners about this gesture. We rarely got a gratitude note from employees' partners about the discretionary bonus amount, but we got plenty of gratitude notes about the small, specific acts of connection that brought meaning.

Gary Yesavage, the past president of Chevron Manufacturing, used to tour his plant and talk to every operator at Christmas. He would go on Christmas Eve to Mass and then onto his tour to show his appreciation. On Christmas day, he would open the presents with the kids, then go back to the plant and shake hands with those on the day shift. Gary gained a tremendous amount of loyalty, respect, caring, and connection because of this practice. I watched him come back to that same plant a few years later to participate in a Visual Management review of the metrics for a maintenance turnaround with approximately 25 employees. Before the presentation, he went around the room and shook hands with everybody, calling them by name. That is a great way to create loyalty and meaning for your employees.

What are small but meaningful things you can do at work to help bring meaning?

3. Create a Significant Emotional Event to show and clarify meaning and purpose.

"You don't give a damn about him, do you, captain?"

Anil Mathur was the CEO of Alaska Tanker Corporation (ATC) for twenty years. During the handover over with the previous CEO back in 2001, he was in the office one day when a call came in that one of his sailors had broken his elbow. As the details came out, Anil heard the captain and others talk about what happened with a tone of, let's get on with it so we can get the cargo to port on time. ATC was having several accidents each month like this. Anil asked the outgoing CEO if he could take this issue on, who said, "With pleasure." Anil had his team get in touch with the captain of the tanker to go to the closest port and come into the Beaverton office to review the accident. The culture on seagoing vessels was that the captain is king, and captains were not asked to leave their ship! In addition, the culture at the time was that delivering on time to the customer was priority one.

The captain did not understand or take too kindly to Anil's request. They would have to dock in Port Angeles, Washington and he would fly to Portland and then drive to the office in Beaverton. What Anil was asking could cost the tanker two days of sailing, and potentially miss the cargo delivery window in Cherry Point, Washington. The captain, realizing that Anil was his boss's boss, had no option but to comply with this order. When the captain got to Beaverton, Anil asked him to wait in the conference room. Anil then told his future direct reports, "No one goes into the conference room until I do." Ninety minutes later, once the captain had some time to contemplate what had happened and being summoned to see the CEO, Anil and the senior team came into the conference room. The captain was worried about delivering the cargo on time, but Anil seemed unconcerned with this priority. He wanted to create a new culture and new meaning for the company. With the entire senior team listening, Anil started a line of questioning to understand what happened. It went like this:

Anil: "Captain, how is the employee that broke his elbow?"

Captain: "Fine. He has a new cast and is feeling fine."

Anil: "Did he make it back home?"

Captain: "Yes."

Anil: "How long will he miss work?"

Captain: "I am not sure. We really need to get back to sea to deliver on time to the port." (Growing impatient).

Anil: (Patiently continued the line of questioning.) "How is his family handling it?"

Captain: "I am not sure. I'm not even sure he has family."

Then Anil saw his chance to change the culture and create new meaning.

Anil: "You just don't give a damn about him, do you?"

Everybody in the room stared at the captain, expecting emotions to get out of control. The captain softened and got the point.

Captain: "I'm sure my HR people do, but I guess I don't. I probably should know that."

They went on to have a great conversation about caring for employees as part of the company's goal. If we care for our employees as Anil so beautifully demonstrated, we will have the results we're looking for. In ATC's case, they can improve safety, take care of the environment, meet customer commitments, and be the company of choice for the Union Hall of Sailors. He instructed the captain to tell everybody on the boat what happened, and to call his fellow captains in the rest of the fleet and tell the story. The story spread like wildfire and a new meaning for ATC was born.

Anil in this way sent a new message and created shared meaning for those employees that taking care of the employees and the environment came before anything else, and that was non-negotiable. The culture and performance change were triggered by this significant emotional event. ATC went on to have nine years without a lost-time accident. Previously, they were averaging one per month. In the 20 years Anil led ATC, they only had one additional lost-time accident. Fleet availability and financial losses from incidents improved dramatically.

Anil went on to implement significant behavioral training over two decades with employees to continue to improve the caring culture and performance. The components included Emotional Intelligence, Wellness, and Mindfulness.

Great leadership makes a difference. Anil says, "A necessary component of successful leadership includes self-expression and a common company-wide value system." Shared meaning makes all the difference.

4. Developing Organizational Meaning and Purpose through off-sites.

As we have discussed, people want to know what they're doing for their career matters. They want to know their work is important and makes a difference to the company, the team, and the boss. I have seen many leaders do a great job annually (and sometimes more often) by taking their team off-site to a hotel or other type of gathering spot outside of the office to create a shared experience to enhance purpose and meaning. I have found that a carefully planned agenda and a carefully planned evening of relaxation and fun can increase meaning that may last the whole year.

"Work hard and Play hard."

James Bowzer used to take his team off-site to create buy-in for the yearly plan and to have some fun with the team. He is a hardworking Nebraska engineer and once he got the chance to lead teams, he became a student of leadership. Once Jim learned an important leadership concept, he took it and ran with it. His yearly off-sites were so valuable and so much fun. The days usually started with an icebreaker for the team to get to know each other. He loved 'two truths and a lie'. Each person took turns sharing two truths and a lie with the team and the team had to guess which one was a lie. They had so much fun with this little exercise. "You learn so much about each person that otherwise you wouldn't have known," Jim would say. The business agendas were carefully planned out to review an important part of leadership and management principles and to have each team member present their yearly plan to the group for feedback and input. The agenda created shared goals and meaning. If corporate was rolling out a new expectation, he wanted his groups to be the best implementers of the new policies. He used these off-sites to roll out new programs and to create buy-in.

One year, some people on his team were struggling with ideas for monthly accountability meetings and finding the right metrics to review. He had Mike Michelis, the "IT Guy", share his metrics. Typically, IT can be one of the more difficult areas to measure, but Mike was not afraid of accountability. Jim would have Mike present first and make sure he got plenty of recognition and reinforcement. At night after dinner, we would also have fun with some kind of group game. One year, it was favorite movie clips from each person and you had to guess whose it was. Often, it was group karaoke. That was not always a pretty sight and sound, but it was fun and it connected the team to a shared meaning and bonding.

If your progress toward your team goals are slower than expected, or worse yet, are being stymied by the team, try increasing the clarity of your teams' 'why' as illustrated in the examples above. Try doing simple things to create meaning and purpose. Management thinker and writer Gary Hamel urges leaders to see themselves as "entrepreneurs of meaning". Of course, if you really want to make the largest difference to your team as a leader, start with your 'why'.

Clarify your own purpose so that you can truly be authentic and powerful to those you lead. How to create and identify your purpose is presented in the next section.

Lessons Learned

For an employee at work

What can I do? I am only an employee - not the boss. Answer: Bring a purpose mindset to work. Bring your purpose to work every day. If your purpose is to be creative, then find creative projects. If your purpose has to do with helping others, then that can be acted out every day. What if you're "just" a front-line worker and don't lead anybody? First of all, you influence everybody around you every day! Secondly, try coming to work with a purpose mindset. Try coming to work with a look at the greater purpose of your work. If you're a teacher, you are developing the workers and parents of the future. If you are an executive assistant, you're helping your boss influence hundreds of people so that they can safely bring your product to market.

You can find meaning and purpose in anything if you bring a purpose mindset. All the research shows that people with purpose have increased job satisfaction and increased health benefits. Bring purpose every day!

SECTION I
Why Purpose

SECTION II
How to Develop Purpose

SECTION III
Plan to Live Your Purpose

SECTION IV
Purposeful Practice

SECTION V
Staying on Purpose

SECTION VI
Purpose at Work

Live Your Purpose

Conclusion

Purposefully Bringing it all Together

As I mentioned in the introduction and shared throughout this book, there is mounting evidence and research that articulating purpose has extreme value in a person and organization's existence. I have also attempted to show how to take that purpose and live your best life.

The design principles to live your best live are:

1. Develop your Purpose and Plan to live it.
2. Practice and implement the plans.
3. Appropriately respond mindfully, gratefully, and based on your values.

Purpose+Planning+Practice+Response = Best Life

Below is the process we have just reviewed to living intentionally and being able to accomplish your purpose and goals.

The Model to Living a Purpose Fulfilled Life

As we have reviewed, there is so much more to living purposefully than just writing a purpose statement. We have reviewed an integrated systems approach to find fulfillment, happiness, and to accomplish our financial, spiritual, physical, career, and relationship goals. If people can understand and practice these skills, tools, and mindset changes, we can achieve our highest potential and live our best life with no regrets.

Continuous Improvement on My Purpose

"An excellent way to identify the values you want to stand for is to go through some kind of purpose-or values-clarification process. I have found nothing more valuable than the creation of a mission statement or credo, whether it be personal, family or organizational. Creating an expression of what you stand for – and living by it – will pay great dividends in helping you become more credible and trusted."

~Stephen M. R. Covey

I n 2005, I modified my Purpose Statement. It now reads:

I will strive for and share the benefits of Continuous Improvement in my life, my families, and those in my circle of influence. I desire my Continuous Improvement efforts to be interdependently benefiting my vocation, avocation, and ecclesiastical service. I desire to live Continuous Improvement with a spirit of love, acceptance, and compassion for others and myself.

I do not believe purpose statements are meant to be changed every year, but they can be tweaked and updated from time to time as new maturity and insights are revealed, created, and learned.

195

The first line in my purpose statement helped me find my career in continuous improvement. The updated first line now compels me to write and share this book with the world. The second line was developed to help the things I'm learning at work to benefit my personal life and those whom I serve, and vice versa. In my coaching and counseling efforts, I have seen the lessons of continuous improvement benefit others. My hobbies of running, biking, and golf have also benefited from continuous improvement. When I was trying to qualify for the Boston Marathon in 2003, I applied every bit of incremental knowledge about continuous improvement to qualify for my age group by 40 seconds. The simple continuous improvement method of PDCA, aka Plan, Do, Check, and Act, was applied during every long run. I had to constantly Check and Act to make small adjustments in clothing, nutrition, and hydration. To endure the over three hours of running at a high pace, I had to trim seconds off each mile to qualify for the marathon. It became very scientific to understand how much "Gu Energy Gel" or hydration of some sort you needed every 30 minutes in order to keep from bonking at the end of the race. Everything you do in the first half of the race is setting you up for a strong finish. There are fantastic learnings from endurance sports; it is a fascinating lesson for Continuous Improvement. There is goal setting, planning, setbacks, overcoming training and race adversity, pain, and injury - all to accomplish a goal and a dream.

The third line or the new line to my purpose statement is probably the most important one to me right now. My mindfulness lessons and feedback from children and others have taught me the importance of showing unconditional love and suspending judgment. The best way to help others (and yourself) is to show love, compassion, and not to judge. This, of course, is a work-in-progress or should I say, continually improving in my life.

I love the continually improving process. The other day, my oldest son came to me and said, "Dad, you're still driven and focused, but you're so much more loving and less judgmental of others." He had no idea that the third line about this had been added to my purpose statement. It was a powerful validation that I was headed toward my 'updated' purpose.

A New Definition of Success:

I hope this book has helped you clarify what success really means to you. A Purpose connected to your values is success. Money isn't success, titles aren't success, your kids winning awards isn't necessarily success. Having more toys than your neighbors isn't even close to success. Working towards happiness and your purpose is success. Being grateful for what you have versus what you don't have, that's success and happiness. Making small progress towards your big dreams and goals, that's success. Just waking up every morning and to keep trying - that's success! Accepting setbacks and learning from them, that is success.

I hope the stories coupled with the research and the step-by-step processes I've shared in this book will help you live your purpose and find true happiness and success. Good luck! If I can help you on your journey to find and live your best self, contact me at rickh@ci4lfe.org.

Live a life with sustainable Continuous Improvement and Live your Purpose! CI4life!

Additional Resources

Weekly Planner. You can go to www.ci4life.org to register for your weekly planning resource that allows you to have your purpose/mission statement in one place along with your roles and goals. From those goals, you develop your weekly plan as outlined in the chapter on goal setting.

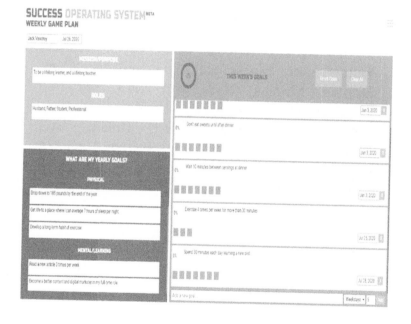

Coaching Services

Sign up for a free coaching session with Rick Heyland on www.ci4life.org. Rick can help you finalize your purpose statement and align them to your goals and weekly planning as outlined.

Acknowledgments

First and foremost, to my wonderful and beautiful wife, Cheryl. People who know me know that she is the glue that holds the team together. Words cannot describe the stability and selfless love she has provided for our big family and me. She is so supportive of my goals and dreams. She has also helped to edit and be my sounding board for this book.

To my six kids (Nicole, Brett, Taylor, Lauren, Tanner, and Mackenzie), five in-laws (Cam, Heather, Morgan, Nick, and J.R.), and 14.5 grandkids (Jaden, Kennedy, London, Maverick, Brookston, Savannah, Parker, Brielle, Eve, Emmeline, John, Jay, Charlie, Tommy, and ???, soon-to-be born), I love you unconditionally. Thank you for your example of living life with purpose and trying to be the best you can be. You inspire me with what you're doing with your kids and with your lives. Thanks for your support and encouragement. Special thanks to Brett for his valuable review of the book and to Mackenzie for her marketing of CI4life and this book.

To my Mom and Dad who taught me to live a purpose filled and goal-filled life. "Work hard and play hard," my mom would say. I love you!

Thanks to my brother, Dr. Daren Heyland, for his expert review of the material. His insights on flow and design were critical to enhance the reader's understanding and experience. Please check out his website here: www.planwellguide.com. **The Plan Well Guide is a tool to help you learn about medical treatments and prepare you for decision-making during a serious illness, like COVID-19 pneumonia. It's about getting the medical care that's right for you or your loved one.**

Additional thanks to John Shewfeldt, Jerry Weisenfelder, Gary Yesavage, Dale Heyland, and Nola Patterson for their feedback and review of the script.

Also, at RLG International, my bosses/mentors, peers, the employees, and our clients. Thanks for everything I have learned from you. It has been my absolute privilege to work with you. I am so grateful for these experiences in my life.

To those leaders and friends who took the time to read the manuscript and provide a recommendation, at first I thought you were talking about somebody else! Your efforts and words inspire me to be better. Thank you!

To the authors and books I have quoted, I hope I have represented your material wisely and properly. Your books have inspired me.

To Jack Vawdrey, my editor, programmer, and marketing content manager for C14life, your coaching on social media platforms has been fantastic. His LinkedIn profile is: https://www.linkedin.com/in/jackvawdrey/

Also, thanks to Marianne, my talented editor. I could have never completed this project without your expertise and guidance.

References

Articles

Alimujiang, A., Wiensch, A., Boss, J., Fleischer, N. L., Mondul, A. M., McLean, K., Mukherjee, B., & Pearce, C. L. (2019). Association Between Life Purpose and Mortality Among US Adults Older Than 50 Years. JAMA network open, *2*(5), e194270. https://doi.org/10.1001/jamanetworkopen.2019.4270

Bonebright, C. A., Clay, D. L., & Ankenmann, R. D. (2000). The relationship of workaholism with work–life conflict, life satisfaction, and purpose in life. *Journal of Counseling Psychology, 47*(4), 469-477.

Bruneau, M. 5 Things Everyone Should Know About Acceptance. Retrieved from https://www.mindbodygreen.com/0-13730/5-things-everyone-should-know-about-acceptance.html

Clarke, T. C., Barnes, P. M., Black, L. I., Stussman, B. J., Nahin, & R. L. (2018). Use of Yoga, Meditation, and Chiropractors Among U.S. Adults Aged 18 and Over. NCHS Data Brief. (325):1-8.

Cohen, R., Bavishi, C., & Rozanski, A. (2016). Purpose in Life and Its Relationship to All-Cause Mortality and Cardiovascular Events: A Meta-Analysis. Psychosomatic Medicine, *78*(2), 122–133. https://doi.org/10.1097/PSY.0000000000000274

Craig, N. & Snook, S.A. (2014). From Purpose to Impact. Harvard Business Review. Retrieved from https://hbr.org/2014/05/from-purpose-to-impact

Cranston, S. & Keller, S. (2013). Increasing the Meaning Quotient of Work, McKinsey Quarterly. Retrieved from https://www.mckinsey.com/business-functions/organization/our-insights/increasing-the-meaning-quotient-of-work#

Debats, D. L., Van der Lubbe, P. M., & Wezeman, F. R. (1993). *On the psychometric properties of the Life Regard Index (LRI): A measure of meaningful life.* Personality and Individual Differences, *14*(2), 337-345.

Kashdan, T., & McKnight, P.E. (2009). Origins of Purpose in Life: Refining our Understanding of a Life Well Lived. Psychological topics, 18, 303-313.

Kerns, C. D. (2006). Gratitude at Work: Counting your blessings will benefit yourself and your organization. Graziado Business Review, *9*(4). Retrieved from https://gbr.pepperdine.edu/2010/08/gratitude-at-work/

Kim, E. S., Strecher, V. J., & Ryff, C. D. (2014). Purpose in life and use of preventive health care services. Proceedings of the National Academy of Sciences of the United States of America, *111*(46), 16331–16336. https://doi.org/10.1073/pnas.1414826111

McKnight, P.E., & Kashdan, T. (2009). Purpose in Life as a System that Creates and Sustains Health and Well-Being: An Integrative, Testable Theory. Review of General Psychology, 13, 242 - 251.

Radcliffe, B. (2019). How did Warren Buffett get started in business? Investopedia. Retrieved from https://www.investopedia.com/ask/answers/081314/how-did-warren-buffett-get-started-business.asp

Rainey, L. (2014). The Search for Purpose in Life: An Exploration of Purpose, the Search Process, and Purpose Anxiety. Master of Applied Positive Psychology (MAPP) Capstone Projects. University of Pennsylvania.

The Science of Gratitude: More Benefits Than Expected; 26 Studies and Counting. *Happier Human*. Retrieved from https://www.happierhuman.com/the-science-of-gratitude/

Blogs

Mira Rakicevic: Meditation Statistics That You Should be Aware of (2/2/2020)

Books

An Astronaut's Guide to Life on Earth: What Going to Space Taught Me About Ingenuity, Determination, and Being Prepared for Anything by Chris Hadfield

Atomic Habits: Tiny Changes, Remarkable Results by James Clear

Crush it - Why Now is the Time to Cash in on Your Passion by Gary Vaynerchuk

The 4-Hour Work Week by Tim Ferris

The Happiness Advantage: The Seven Principles That Fuel Success and Performance at Work by Shawn Achor

The Happiness Trap: How to Stop Struggling and Start Living: A Guide to ACT by Russ Harris

High Performance Habits by Brendon Burchard

The How of Happiness: A Scientific Approach to Getting the Life You Want by Sonja Lyubomirsky

How to Measure Your Life by Clayton Christensen

Leading with Gratitude: Eight Leadership Practices for Extraordinary Business Results by Adrian Gostick and Chester Elton

Make Your Bed: Little Things That Can Change Your Life and Maybe Change Your World by Admiral William H. McRaven

Man's Search for Meaning by Viktor Frankl

Mindfulness: An Eight-Week Plan for Finding Peace in a Frantic World by Danny Penman and Mark Williams

The One Minute Manager by Ken Blanchard

Personality Isn't Permanent by Philip Hardy, PhD

The Power of Habit by Charles Duhigg

The Power of Now: A Guide to Spiritual Enlightenment by Eckhart Tolle

Published - The Proven Path from Blank Page to Published Author by Chandler Bolt

7 Habits of Highly Effective People by Dr. Stephen R. Covey

Shot Happens by Mike Schlappi

Small Steps That Can Change Your Life - The Kaizen Way by Dr. Robert Maurer

The Speed of Trust by Stephen M. R. Covey

Success Principles by Jack Canfield

Talent is Overrated by Geoff Colvin

The Three Alarms by Eric Partaker (forthcoming)

The Top Five Regrets of the Dying by Bronnie Ware

What Color Is Your Parachute by Richard Bolles

Podcasts

Continuous Improvement 4 Life with Rick Heyland

- Nathan Goodfellow (2/27/2020)

- Chris Hadfield (3/13/2019)

- Dr. Bob Maurer (4/10/2020)

- Mike Schlappi (3/27/2020)

SPI podcast with Pat Flynn

10% Happier with Dan Harris